LIVING WITH

Emetophobia . . .

MY STORY

LIVING WITH
Emetophobia . . .
MY STORY

CAROLINE DOWDALL

AuthorHouse™
1663 Liberty Drive
Bloomington, IN 47403
www.authorhouse.com
Phone: 1-800-839-8640

First published by AuthorHouse   07/13/2011

ISBN: 978-1-4567-8716-5 (sc)
ISBN: 978-1-4567-8718-9 (hc)
ISBN: 978-1-4567-8717-2 (ebk)

Printed in the United States of America

Any people depicted in stock imagery provided by Thinkstock are models, and such images are being used for illustrative purposes only.
Certain stock imagery © Thinkstock.

This book is printed on acid-free paper.

DEDICATION

Dedicated to Anthony, Phillip and Tim, With love to Billy, Harry and Chloe and to my Darling Husband John . . . Thankyou Darling I love You x

FOREWORD

LIVING WITH MY PHOBIA

Living with my phobia and trying to keep it a secret for the last 46 years has probably been the hardest thing I have ever had to do. Now I wouldn't go as far as to say that it has ruined my life but it has had a massive impact.

You are probably wondering what on earth I am talking about. Spiders or the dark perhaps, no, none of the easy ones or the most discussed ones, I have a huge phobia of vomiting myself and also of others vomiting around me, just in case it is due to an infectious bug that I could contract.

I have only confessed to my own mother in the last few weeks, in fact I know when it was that I told her, it was this Christmas just passed. Relaxed after a couple of drinks we just started chatting and suddenly I found myself telling my mum my inner most dark secrets.

Now to anyone who doesn't suffer and I mean suffer from this phobia it must all seem rather stupid and that was the way I have felt for many years, however for those of you out there who find yourself reading this because you do have the same fear I just hope I can give just a glimmer of hope, but as you know and I know I will be burdened with this for the rest of my life as I think after so many years adapting it will be hard to change my ways.

If just one of the following situations applies to anyone reading my story, trust me it may just help. I used to scour women's magazines hoping to come across such a story looking for answers, looking for some help or idea's how to deal with it, normally all the columnist would reply was that there were professional people out there willing to give help and to seek advice from these so called councillors. I reckon I have only ever found a couple of letters on the subject and amazingly and quite recently on the Jeremy Kyle show there was a young woman who had the same phobia and it was ruining her life with her children as she couldn't cope if they were sick. I found myself staring at the television screen with tears pouring down my face as I felt every ounce of her agony. It was that poor young woman that inspired me to get my life out into the open just to show other sufferers that they are not alone.

Please don't feel that I am miserable though . . . . now I have a fantastic life as I feel now more in control, I will take you through many true scenarios that I have got myself through and how I cope with my life day by day.

MY STORY . . .

Who knows how a phobia starts . . . and what eventually turns it into a life controlling fear. I can remember exactly the day as if it was yesterday when mine started. I must have been about eight years old and my sister was aged five, it was during the long summer holidays and we were both off from school.

Both of our parents happened to work full-time, my father a police officer and my mother in a local factory so my sister and I used to spend the days with our grandparents.

At the time my aunty and uncle were staying with my grandparents, as my aunty was heavily pregnant with her second child. They had recently travelled back to the UK for her to give birth as they were living in Portugal where my uncle had work commitments and back in the 1960's Portugal was not the place where you would want to have a baby. She was hoping for a home birth and I can still remember my Nan's neighbour who lived on the floor above, she lived in a block of flats in Southampton. Was a midwife and on hand to assist with the delivery.

Ok back to the fateful day and the start of my fear . . . .

We had been to Southbourne beach for the day and had spent a wonderful time paddling, building sandcastles and catching crabs in the rock pools finishing the day with a picnic. My uncle had the use of a car and so my Nan, aunty and uncle, young cousin, as well as my sister and myself all squashed into the car for our day's outing. Of course back in those day's seatbelts and the rules of the road were pretty much non-existent which was just as well really as my Nan had to sit in the front sometimes taking my cousin on her lap. My uncle was driving and my aunty sat in the back with me next to her and my sister on the other side of me.

It was on our homeward journey and we were no more than a mile from my Nan's flat when it all started. We were almost home but my cousin was tired and started to cry. She wanted her mum and kept making a fuss bouncing up and down on my aunty's huge pregnant belly. As we were almost home we all tried to ignore her when suddenly my aunty said she was going to be sick . . . . and with that she just managed to get hold of a beach towel before she threw up all over the back of the car. I can remember the smell and desperately wanting to get out of the car. However at the time we were on a main road and had to carry on to the next lay-by.

I cannot recall the make or model of the car but what I can remember is that it only had two doors and the windows in the back of the car were those funny little push out ones. For me and my sister there simply was no escape.

We finally came to a halt where my uncle took my cousin from my aunty as she tried to clean herself up a little, but he would not let us get out of the car as we were only a few minutes from home. I can still feel the absolute desperation that was almost taking hold of my body and mind. Panic filled me and a feeling of immense urgency that I really had to just get away from this situation. I think had I been able to get out of the car I would have probably just taken to my heels and run the rest of the way home rather than get back into the car. I remember trying to occupy my younger sister by watching the reflections of cars in a huge factory window on the opposite side of the road, anything to try and blot out what was really going on.

That for me, was the beginning of my life sentence, not that I blame anyone it just simply evolved.

*   *   *

Now I must have been going to school for a good three years by the time this had happened and can't recall not enjoying it although my mum has said that I used to be the only one crying when I came out of the classroom.

So I can't really say that I have any bad memories of infant school but suddenly, as if my senses had been awakened I now found myself watching my school friends for any particular situation to arise. I became careful who I sat next to, listened to them talking in the playground about who was or had been sick. It always seemed to be a fascinating subject amongst them. For me it was to become a source of mental anguish. By now school for me had now become a bit of an ordeal and going every day was to become my next hurdle.

*   *   *

I bet anyone reading this will recall at some time in their schooldays the assembly first thing in the morning. We would all gather in the school hall in front of the headmaster, sing the usual hymn. "Morning

3

has broken." I can still remember the large word sheets that were projected onto the classically painted white wall to ensure that everyone kept up with the singing. I used to be fascinated by these sheets, this one in particular as it was decorated with huge ladybirds, butterflies and flowers, I never even thought in those days who had painted those, I just used to love them.

Now it was always seemed to be at the quietest part of the service when we were saying our prayers that it used to happen, and it always seemed to happen near to where I was standing . . . . you would suddenly hear a shuffle of feet then that awful splattering sound as someone threw up their breakfast. Of course no-one was allowed to move until the caretaker had come in with a bucket of sawdust and covered the offending mess, leaving a mound that everyone had to silently walk past. So when we were told to bow our heads and say our silent prayers, my prayer always used to be 'Please dear god. Please do not to let anyone be sick near me'. It never seemed to work. Funny enough neither did my prayer work for a baby brother!.

*   *   *

At break time before going out into the playground for a run around the whole class used to have to sit and drink our small bottles of milk. I can guarantee that at least one child would down his or her milk and then projectile vomit across the classroom. I doubt very much that in those days, a child unfortunate to suffer intolerance to dairy products had even been heard of to say the least. Even so I used to dread this time of the morning and oddly even today I never drink milk. Just a drip in my tea and that's it . . . .

*   *   *

Oh and joy of joys came dinnertime . . . . once again in the 1960's a packed lunch was out of the question. It was school dinners or home.

I used to hate Monday mornings when my mum used to hand me two half crowns wrapped in a handkerchief to pay for my dinners. The misery of knowing I had to endure a whole week of what if or maybe the person next to me might be sick. I could hardly get the food eaten half the time, but we were blessed with a big grumpy dinner-lady and

I can still feel the knuckle of her third finger prodding my spine as I miserably sat and forced myself to swallow the food on my plate. I was always the last to finish where oddly you would have thought that I would have finished my food in record time just to get out of the dining hall.

* * *

I remember one school where we used to have to stand and sing "We plough the fields and Scatter. the good seeds on the ground" before filing down to the dinner hall which invariably was the same hall that we had attended assembly in that morning. While queuing up for my dinner I would scour the floor until I spotted the patch where the early morning vomit had lain so I knew what table to avoid . . . anyway I digress . . . . when singing this hymn I could feel my stomach churning and I used to fight the urge to retch as you could bet your last penny I would be on the table where the child would eat his or her dinner and then sick it all back up over the table. What amazed me that none of the other children seemed bothered, they used to laugh and point at the offending child and make the obvious 'uurrrggghhhhh' noises.

I couldn't understand how they could inspect the mess on the table. All I wanted to do was to run away out into the playground.

What we had to do, was, do as the dinner ladies told us to and that was to carefully pick up our plates and go and finish our dinner on a different table. Well that was ok as long as none of the sick had landed on your plate.

I can only think that it was my constant moaning and crying about having schools dinners that prompted my parents to arrange for us to have our lunch with my Nan as she lived a stone's throw from the school and although it was probably boiled mince and potatoes most days I didn't care.

* * *

I know I couldn't ever tell my mum why I hated dinners, even at the age of 9 or so years old. I thought she wouldn't understand me . . . . it was horrible and I am sure this may have sometimes affected me and my enjoyment of my school days.

Ironically though, one of my choices of employment when my youngest child was only about six years was to be a school cook. I felt safe in my cocoon of the kitchen. There was no reason for me to have to go anywhere near the tables used for the dinners as there were dinner ladies that used to deal with the same problems of vomiting children only it was 30 years later.

As the catering staff after the lunchtime was over it was usual that we all used to sit and have a couple of rolls to eat and a cup of coffee for our lunch and the topic of conversation always used to come back to the same subject . . . . how many kids had puked that lunchtime and how many were in the sick bay.I used to get up and start the washing up, and unless they ever get to read this book then they will never ever know I couldn't even bear to hear them talking about it, but in a funny kind of way I was jealous that they could.

*   *   *

Most of my vomit memories are short but weirdly they are etched in my head, which is dreadfully sad. I can recall the events with amazing clarity as if they only happened yesterday, but ask me what happened when my children were young and what good times we had and sadly I cannot recall many happy times.

Ask me about the times when they were sick and I will recount the events again, as if they happened yesterday.

My children, as adults, seem to have better memories of their childhood more than I do and if they happen to talk about a particular event I have to pretend that I do remember. It makes me want to cry sometimes as I honestly feel as if I have totally blocked out a lot of their childhood simply because I was too occupied with the fear of them vomiting. I would give everything and anything to have their time all over again. To be a proper mother to them and not freak out, panic and recoil in disgust if they cried saying they didn't feel well.

*   *   *

So, what do I remember about my own child hood. As I have mentioned, my parents worked. On one particular non-school day I remember another of my aunties was coming to care for us in our home bringing our cousin with her. Now I know I must have been nine years old as I can still remember the house. We did move from this house by the time I was ten.

My parents had already left for work and I was instructed to wait by the window with my younger sister and watch for my aunty to come in the back gate . . . When she arrived my sister started to cry and said her tummy hurt. next thing she was being sick in the kitchen sink and all I wanted to do was to just get away into the garden. I always got this incredible feeling where I had to run away and not be anywhere near to the situation.

I hated the sound that she made when vomiting and that horrible smell. Once free in the garden I stayed out all day . . . . unfortunately it must have been some sort of tummy bug as I woke up later that night and as much as I tried to stop it I vomited in my bed.

In my youth I didn't know what bugs were I blamed the fact I had eaten jelly and peanut butter sandwiches for my tea and to this day I cannot eat peanut butter although give me a bag of peanuts and I will eat the lot.

*   *   *

Now you may understand this or you may think hmmm gone a bit too far but as children we had the usual pets, I laugh to think of it now but I couldn't even stand it if the cat started to cough up her fur balls, as soon as her body started to convulse I would either get out of the room and yell at my parents in sheer panic, or in extreme cases would chase the poor thing around the room desperate to get it out in the garden as I knew wherever she would deposit the mess I would not be able to go back in that room.

If you could see me now though, all these years later I have 6 dogs all of whom throw up now and then. I actually can stand and watch them now, and I do as I am concerned as to what they have tried to eat that may have disagreed with them. I can pick up the mess they make quite easily. Inside the house or outside it doesn't even turn my stomach. Mentally I know that it will not make me ill, but it's also proof to me that I am a lot better than I was as a child.

*   *   *

Another time I can recall being out with my parents on a rare treat, I don't know where we were but I do know we stopped in a lovely old town as we needed to use the toilet.

The public toilets were on a huge island in the middle of the road but you had to go down a long flight of steps to find the ladies.

There was a lady sat on a bench with her young son not far from the stairs and I remember my mum asking if she was alright, apparently she had come over feeling ill while shopping and was resting but I heard her say she felt very sick. Looking back, for all I know she could have been in the early stages of pregnancy or anything really, so . . .

Leaving her there my mum, sister and myself went down to the ladies to use the toilet and all the time I was praying and getting awful butterflies about how was I going to walk past her to get back to the car . . . the feeling again of being trapped was awful but what could I say to my mum . . . . and yes you guessed it, by the time we had got to the top of the steps she had a pile of vomit at her feet and horror of horrors my mum stopped to talk to her and at the same time keeping a tight grip of my hand.

Oh how I wanted just to get away and back to the safety of the car but with a main road to cross there was no way I could escape, I just kept looking the other way until the woman insisted she would be ok.

Public toilets over the years have proved problem areas on more than one occasion. Why is it I have managed to pick the one where once again someone has used then to be sick in but not cleaned up . . . . more about this topic later . . .

*   *   *

The dentist was another of my horror's as a child and still is now. I am not sure whether it was because of my fear of being sick but I had the most sensitive of gag reflexes. I would start to retch even before the poor man had managed to get anywhere near my mouth. I couldn't stand the suction tube being left in my mouth and used to starve myself hours if not days before a visit to the dentist as I really thought that if he kept making me retch eventually I would be sick. So it all became a battle when I was a child and I couldn't wait for the day when I was an adult and could choose for myself to visit the dentist or not. As it was I did have poor teeth as a child and had to endure many fillings. I will admit that I avoided going to the dentist for many years in my early adulthood and it was only when I saw a picture of me, actually it was a home video of me talking and smiling that I suddenly felt very ashamed at what I saw. Spurred on by the vision of my teeth on this film I booked to see my dentist to have some treatment. I did warn him I was one of life's worst patients to which he laughed but in a nice way and said most people feared the dentist, I don't think he bargained for what a nightmare patient I was going to be though. As soon as he went to inspect my teeth I had to resist the urge to push his hands out of the way. I eventually explained about my gag reflex working overtime and try as he might it became such a distressing time for both of us, I ended up by getting hold of his hands and pushing him as hard as I could. Eventually he agreed I did have a problem and arranged for me to be sedated on a different visit then sent me home feeling very humble.

The sedation worked quite well and the dentist managed to get the impressions he needed for my crowns but I could still recall the fact that even though I was very heavily drugged I could still feel myself gagging but was unable to do anything about it.

As for visiting the dentist now I do push myself to visit but given the choice I would not go at all as I still have a very bad reflex and struggle even when cleaning my teeth and worse still living in a foreign country (Spain) how do I explain to the dentist that I can't cope with all the equipment that has to be put inside my mouth that will render me a gibbering wreck fighting the urge not to be sick.

*   *   *

1972 and at last I could leave school, I do recall that the last couple of years at school were probably my best. The traditional assembly had ceased and as we were all 15 years old we were more in control of ourselves and if anyone felt ill they usually had the grace to excuse themselves to the matron, thinking back most of the sickness was usually the result of a hangover . . . . usually on a Friday morning, after the Thursday night trip to the youth club to watch Top of the pops. Some of the older boys and the more promiscuous of the girls used to then sit around in the cemetery opposite the school grounds sharing bottles of whatever alcohol they could take from their parent's drinks cabinets or get from the local off-licence. I used to think they looked so cool and grown up I was jealous.

Looking back thankfully for me I wouldn't drink as I was too scared of being sick and the same goes for smoking. I can remember going to the local park where some of the other kids had managed to obtain some cigarettes. I used to endure a lot of teasing about not being good enough or grown up enough to smoke but the sheer possibility that it would make me sick was so strong that I bluntly refused and to this day I never smoked.

I remember my dad telling me a story of how when he was very young he managed to get his hands on some woodbines
. . . . tucked away in his bedroom he smoked the lot and then panicked as he felt very ill. Now we are going back to the late 1930's early 1940's and my grandparents had a very basic house which had been in the bomb zone during the war . . . . no bathroom but a tin bath hanging on the wall and an outside loo complete with wooden seat . . . so with no chance of a quiet dash to the bathroom my poor dad ended up filling his wellington boots !!! . . . . didn't put him off though as I remember him smoking when I was quite young but glad to say has given up all together now.

*   *   *

Another time I was invited to a party. I was still at school but at 14 ¾'s years old thinking but I was 18 I wanted to be seen to be allowed to go.

Probably against my parent's wishes, they somehow agreed to me attending this party.

It was to be held in the village hall for someone's birthday and a boy I thought was the top dollar and probably the school heart-throb, asked me to go with him. My dad insisted he took me and insisted on collecting me so I said I would see him there. He was to me a bit of a wild child although his parents were respectable people he revelled in his rebellion . . . wore his hair long at school, turned up in a denim jacket. So I was some-what gobsmacked that he asked to see me. What I didn't expect was for him to get completely drunk and more or less pass out within the first hour . . . his mates lined up some wooden chairs along the wall and laid him down facing the wall where he promptly emptied the gallons of drink from his stomach all over the hall floor . . . . I phoned my dad to come and get me as I couldn't bear to be around the other partygoers who all looked as if they may throw up at any given moment.

*   *   *

Even now when I visit the UK my three sons always have a get together and insist that I come out to the local pub for a few drinks. This for them is a fun evening with maybe a few games of pool or darts. For me it's becomes my nightmare as I am more interested of the antics of the other pub-goers and how much they are all drinking. Technically it is none of my business, but having to endure going to the ladies toilets and worrying needlessly about whether or not any of the young girls would be vomiting in there spoiled for me what should have been a simple evening out with my sons.

Ok . . . . Before you read on I do want to assure you this book is not just a book about stories of people being sick all the time, I am just trying to explain how I feel my phobia seemed to accelerate out of control so quickly.

As you already know at this stage nobody knew or had the slightest idea of my fear and therefore I didn't tell anyone. I was fantastic at making excuses and sadly I know I missed out on a lot of things . . . by my own choice I will add . . . . things like school trips. Why ??? Well just in case someone was ill on the coach.

*   *   *

I have only just told my husband . . . . who happens to work away from home, that I am trying to write a sort of life journal, as a help to others. He was amazed to learn that I had this phobia and as we have been married for 7 years he told me he would never have guessed so I suppose that proves that I have taught myself to cope. He also said to me. "There are many reasons why people are sick and it's natural and sometimes really funny" . . . and then proceeded to tell me some stories to make me laugh, all are true and although at the time I thought YUEECHH . . . . I did actually laugh with him so I will share them

11

with you and hope you too can laugh at them without recoiling in horror.

OK, here is the first of his funny stories.

When my husband was at his junior school which just happened to be Roman Catholic school there was a morning when Mass was actually held at the school in the hall . . . . and like I mentioned there was always someone who would be sick. Well his school pal whom shall be called Mr P was that person, but the poor lad managed to catch the offending mess in his hands and pushed it back into his mouth and swallowed it again. why?? because otherwise he would have got the strap for making a noise and mess during the all important Mass . . . . obviously to you and me it sounds gross but the way he told it and how he described all the lads desperately trying not to laugh out loud, as we know what boys can be like I had to agree and laugh with him.

Well I hope you had a little titter at that as disgusting as it is. I do have a couple of others which I will slot in when you are least expecting it !

*   *   *

So, having managed to complete my schooling I was fortunate to land myself a job in the local bank. Luckily back in 1972 it was normal to go straight from school to work with great thanks to the career's advisor.

It was all pretty uneventful and I didn't have any cause for my phobia to kick in until one of the ladies became pregnant and suffered from morning sickness. As a junior my part of the office was right at the back next to the staff kitchen and toilets. I know it wasn't her fault but every time I saw her rushing my way with her hand over her mouth I used to first get a horrible hot and cold feeling quickly followed by the strong urge to get as far away as possible . . . . I think it's called 'the flight of fear' . . . . so I would make any excuse to be away from my work station and then not only that I couldn't bring myself to go anywhere near to the toilet in the office and therefore stopped drinking and eating very much so I wouldn't need to use it all day . . . . I was 16 years old, 6ft tall and probably weighed only 9 stone.

*   *   *

My biggest nightmare in the bank happened a few years later when I had progressed to being a cashier. It was the run up to Christmas, in fact it was Christmas Eve and we were due to finish at 12 o'clock lunchtime. We were extremely busy and a lot of our customers had already started drinking as you could smell it when they talked.

I had already noticed a very drunk looking man in the queue and was praying that he wouldn't come to me, but of course he did and to my horror started to be sick from his drink in front of me and some of the vomit ended up in my serving tray . . . . if you recall the serving trays have a scooped shape so without going into massive detail it was just revolting.

All I can remember is getting off my chair as fast as I could and thank god one of the supervisors cleared the mess with great efficiency whilst some other customer took the man back outside. However that wasn't the end of my nightmare as we all had to leave the building by the same door that the customers use and I spent the rest of the morning praying that he hadn't thrown up outside.

*   *   *

I don't know really at what age I found myself constantly scouring the pavements when out shopping for evidence of any vomit patches, probably I did it subconsciously from a young age, but I know if I spotted one I still got that awful hot and cold feeling and would cross the road rather than walk past it. I would look at people and if I saw anyone bending over as if to be sick, the stupid thing here is, there may have been nothing wrong with them they could have been tying a shoelace for all knew, but in my head I just couldn't be sure . . . . or looking as if they may be ill I would either turn around and walk the other way or cross the road. In shops I always watched people and tried to avoid being around people as much as possible . . . . when food shopping I would check the isles first to see how many people were in that isle and also check the floor to see if it was clean. It used to be a nightmare because not only did I have this ritual but also trying to avoid anyone who may have been carrying a sickness bug . . . . HOW THE HELL WOULD I KNOW ???? . . . . it was just horrible and getting out of control.

*   *   *

So now I am a working 16 year old and I had a boyfriend, we used to go out in the evenings for a drink and my favourite tipple was sherry . . . . which really was my introduction to alcohol . . . . I knew too much would make me ill and there was no way that was going to happen, but I did on one occasion under estimate the strength of the drink and the warmth of a log fire. I fought against being sick, refused to be sick but felt ill for days and to this day I will fight against it but you will learn as we go along what else I resorted to when trying to cope.

*   *   *

As my boyfriend worked for an airline company we were sometimes lucky enough to be offered a trip. One Christmas we had the opportunity to go to Jersey for the day, we were to take a coach to the airport and then a flight to Jersey . . . . nothing difficult in that except some of the fellow passengers had all been out the night before and turned up for the coach very much the worse for wear. I wanted to get off there and then . . . . my heart was racing as I looked at them, my mouth was dry my 'flight of fear ' feeling took over and I was desperate to get off the coach, using all excuses that I didn't feel well and didn't want to go . . . . no chance the driver got on. I was literally paralysed with fear and that was only the start of the nightmare journey . . . . we stopped several times for these guys to get off and throw up, even worse one of them sat near us had to use his friends handkerchief to vomit in and all this took me straight back to being trapped inside the car with my aunty some 8 years ago . . .

The sad thing is that since that day I have avoided coaches as much as possible, if there were any works outings say for Christmas or any organised outings I would always find an excuse for us not to go unless we could take our own car. Which now as I look back was very selfish on my part as I wouldn't be the one to be driving and therefore expecting my partner to accept the fact of not drinking all night whilst our friends and colleagues were having a great time, but the thought of just one of those people on the same coach just having too much to drink and being ill on the coach would have played on my mind all night, had we gone on the coach, so it was easier to say no.

I used to look at holidays longingly but if it included a coach transfer then forget it, so holidays abroad were not an option.

Ok so back to the trip to Jersey. Having finally made the coach journey we were ready to board the plane I waited and watched to see where the 'thrower uppers' sat so I could at least avoid them allowing myself to relax a little What I didn't bargain for was that the lady to my left was going to be so ill, mainly due to our very turbulent flight. She was filling up the sick bags as fast as the stewardess could supply them it was horrible, mainly as I was trapped in my seat. I couldn't run away, in fact I was totally powerless to do anything except put my fingers in my ears and stare out of the window praying that the flight would just end.

*   *   *

Thinking back it didn't stop me going on one more trip when once again my boyfriends company offered a four day trip to West Berlin. The wall dividing the East and West of Berlin was still up then. It was an amazing trip, there was a group of about 12 of us and the well travelled amongst them were fascinating with their knowledge of the country I have to say and my eyes were opened up to what travel could teach you it was wonderful . . . until the fateful journey home.

I will never know to this day what caused it but the morning of the day we were to travel home my boyfriend didn't come down for breakfast so I went to find him . . . . I discovered him in his room feeling very ill and the panic that consumed me at that time was unbelievable. All I could think was that we had a coach trip from the hotel to the airport, a plane journey and then another coach trip from the airport back to our home town. As if on cue he started to vomit and I fled his room . . . I can remember pleading with his friends if they would go and get him and deal with him on the journey home, but of course they just laughed and said he would get over it and was the German beer.

Of course we did get home but it sealed my fate once and for all and from that day forward at the age of 16 years I never got on a plane again and wasted the next 30 years of opportunities . . . .

*   *   *

If I look back at my life I now see that by the age of 17 I have consciously and sub-consciously given up my options of travel by plane, coach or bus, and without even realising this eventually progressed to trains. The feeling of not being in control of my environment was pretty much, too much to comprehend. I am not even sure as to why the train travel crept in but I can remember reading snippets of news in the local papers about the late night drunks that used to catch the last train home and would make the headlines for fighting on the train and there would always be the line that I would read at least 5 times . . . . vomiting in the carriage, on the floor and over the seats . . . yuck, there was no way I would get on that train. So it was by car or walk as far as I was concerned.

*   *   *

So I think it's time for one of my husband's little stories . . . .

His father is fond of a whiskey now and then, however his mum does pour rather large one's . . . . anyway he had rather too much and was very poorly the next day. He laid on the sofa looking very green around the gills and found it a struggle to get to bathroom if he was going to be ill. so in desperation my husband's mum went to the kitchen, found a strong carrier bag and fastened it around his ears so it resembled something like a horses nose bag . . . . funnily enough as the day progressed the more he filled it the nearer his head got to the floor . . . . I laugh at the thought of it as he is such a quiet unassuming man and to visualise him like this is just so funny . . . . even I can laugh at that one if I don't think of the carrier bag!

*   *   *

So here I am at 17 years old I don't enjoy going out for a social drink with my boyfriend as if we meet with his friends they always wanted to be in the public side, not being a snob but that was always the side where the younger people used to be playing darts, a game of pool or generally out for a good time and invariably getting very drunk, and realistically why shouldn't they, it was a Friday night and they had been paid, it was their life and they were having in their eyes a good night out, for me it was a living nightmare.

I used to watch them like a hawk, waiting for them to go outside to throw up the vast quantities of ale or make it to the gents. The feeling of being trapped was always there.

I will add here that thankfully my boyfriend wasn't a huge drinker and given that he also had a car in the car park I was spared that ordeal from him.

I used to dread going out on a Friday and was thrilled at the age of 17 when we decided to get married, much to my parents horror as my boyfriend was a whole 6 years older than me and had been my only boyfriend, but to me at least it meant we had to stay in every night to save our money thus curtailing the need to frequent places where my nightmares could be exploited, with the excuse of saving for our wedding.

In my head I felt in control for the first time having found my way of dealing with living with my secret hell. I could turn down any offers of any trips out, certainly any social gatherings were out, "Sorry can't really afford it as I am getting married" was probably the most used line of speech that I used for the next 2 years. I had mastered the art of shopping by choosing the empty isles, and even those trips were limited to the weekends where I would be cocooned in the safety of my boyfriend's car from the house to the car park of the shop thus not having to walk too far where I may just have to avoid a vomit patch on the pavement.

We spent our courting time mostly at his mother's house watching TV, or at my parents doing much the same, going out walking in the country and as I was the eldest daughter and the first probable headache for my parents I still had to be home by 10pm, up until my wedding day.

If asked where we were going for our honeymoon I quite happily announced that we had managed to buy our own home and didn't need to go away, secretly I dreamed of palm trees, sugar white sands and the romance of it all, which was made too clear for me when a work colleague of mine got married a few months before me. Her photographs that she proudly bought into work looked magical, I wanted to cry knowing I would never be able to do the same and the only way to stop was to imagine getting on the coach and the plane. It did the trick.

*   *   *

Now you will probably wonder by now if I was ever ill, did I ever vomit and I can say with hand on heart, the Last time that I could recall being sick was that night all those years ago in my bed the time when I gave up eating peanut butter sandwiches ! . . . . until one day at work and I must still be 17 years old, so a massive gap of at least 8 or 9 years.

My weekly treat on a Friday was to go the fish and chip in the high street for my lunch.

On this particular day I decided on a steak and kidney pie rather than fish, it tasted lovely and I was none the wiser until I started to get a niggling pain in the centre of my stomach. It stayed for the rest of the day and at the time I thought maybe I was due my monthly period. I even went home and I can remember to this day that my mother had got home from work before me and as usual she would cook our evening meal and if I was later than usual she would put it on a saucepan of boiling water to keep warm . . . no such luxuries as a microwave in those days. As normal Friday supper was always fish, mash potato and peas topped with parsley sauce . . . . isn't it so weird that I can vividly remember such trivial things.

With the pain still there I ate my meal as normal as I felt fine and was looking forward to seeing my boyfriend later that evening.

However around 8 o'clock that night my nightmare began and however much I tried to fight it I eventually became very ill and as the fear engulfed me my body totally took over as I had contracted food poisoning from my lunchtime pie. This time I could not fight it I could not control the vomiting I was ill for four days . . . my parents were fantastic in looking after me but even they didn't know about my problems then and the mental anguish I was going through . . . . as you might guess I do not eat meat pies unless I have cooked them personally.

*   *   *

Life for me in all honesty was pretty much uneventful. Our wedding went off without any glitches, no-one got overly drunk and suddenly here I am at the age of 19 years old married, and feeling in control and I must probably point out that at this time I didn't even know that there was such a thing as a "vomiting phobia" to me it was just something that I hated to witness but having eliminated the situations that would render me in any way threatened life for me was good. I had friends at work, no-one was pregnant, I had a job away from the counter so I could stay at my desk, head in my ledger books and shut the world out as far as I was concerned. I could control what I ate or rather how much as there was always the 'just in case' niggle in my head, that, just in case I did eat something bad there wouldn't be very much in my stomach for me to bring up, so I ate like a mouse I suppose, no wonder I was a size zero, although in those days 1977 to be precise a size zero was not even heard of. I used to get called Twiggy and the joke used to be, stand sideways and you disappear.

*   *   *

After a year of being married the maternal instinct started to kick in and for a while this feeling of wanting a baby took over my thinking completely so without much consideration and looking any further ahead into my life very much caught up in the romance of it all I found myself pregnant within a couple of months. Ecstatic at having it confirmed I attended my first chat with the midwife and she explained the routine of monthly check ups, the blood tests and the problems I should be aware of and how to deal with morning sickness !. Something I hadn't even bargained for when all I could think of was a cute, sweet smelling baby in my arms and not what I could possibly have to endure to get there.

*   *   *

Luckily for me I didn't suffer at all, but in my head there was the thought that I might be and so I at my next visit begged them to give me some tablets to take to stop me being sick even though I wasn't, and stupidly I took these pills every day so I knew that I wouldn't be ill. BUT I WAS NOT SUFFERING ANYWAY, it was just for my peace of mind.

I read every text book about pregnancy until I was convinced that I would be safe to stop these pills, around the 5 months, but kept them to hand just in case . . . As I read my books I began to relax and enjoy being pregnant, was still careful as to how much I ate as I had read that as the baby grew it would put pressure on the stomach area but, still in control I made it through the nine months, felt fantastic that I had survived it all without the need to be sick and congratulated myself on a perfect pregnancy and amongst the new friends I had made at the antenatal clinic I was a role model, had not gained too much weight, hadn't suffered any sickness as most of them had, but none of them were aware of the lengths I had gone to.

*   *   *

So by now we were all due to give birth and we were shown a birthing film to prepare us for the event, so you can imagine my despair even the 'flight of fear' kicked in when the poor woman on the film vomited during a contraction. The midwife then cheerfully announced in her sing song (let's patronise all of you terrified looking nine month pregnant ladies)that it was quite common for mummy to be sick when having the baby, but like the pain it's all soon forgotten when you have your bundle of joy in your arms. I was mortified, here I was having got through it all and now faced once again with my nightmare and this one I couldn't avoid as the poor little mite had to get out !! . . . . As my friends gave birth I couldn't wait to see them, not to see them personally or the baby but to conduct my little unknown survey on who was sick and if by any chance any of them weren't so I could assess what the odds were of me being a sickly one . . . . even as I sit here now typing this I want to cry, it all seems so pointless now but at that time it was vital for me to know.

*   *   *

The birth was actually fine, I think I concentrated so much on not wanting to be sick that it took my mind off of any pain and I had a wonderful natural birth, I was for now the happiest person in the world. I had 10 days ahead of me cosseted in my hospital bed, a cute little bundle of joy, a sweet little boy, and when visited by my friends who were still to go through the birthing process I couldn't wait to say how wonderful it all was.

It's quite funny really as when faced with the fear and nothing happens I get a huge adrenalin rush as I feel I have crossed a milestone and feel fantastic.

*   *   *

Now as we know all babies sick up a little milk when winded and that actually didn't bother me, I knew it was nothing contagious, so I would cheerfully mop up his pukes and think nothing of it.

I settled into a glorious routine of being a perfect mum, I could cope with my life, having eaten mouse size meals I was back in my size twelve jeans within a couple of weeks.I was still in control of when and if I ate, whether this contributed to not being able to breastfeed my baby properly I will never know but I chose the option of that he was just a hungry baby and within a couple of weeks he was being bottle fed.

I had the pram so I walked everywhere, I couldn't drive but a couple of times a week I used to go to the shops and having a new baby and pram to focus on I didn't have time to think about looking out for vomit patches on the pavements or bother too much about people in general although I think I was so used to my odd routine It happened naturally anyway.

Afternoons were spent with my group of new mum's, we used to take it in turns to visit each other's houses to compare notes and at 21 years old I felt on top of the world. I could even look at the other babies even when they burped up a little congealed milk it didn't bother me.

How it was all to change though . . . . By the time my son was a year old he was eating proper food and was running around, he was a little person now. A typical youngster picking up bits off the floor and everything went into his mouth as he was teething.

*   *   *

On one particular day I had visited my mother in law, as my husband was working nights, we had a lovely day, by 6pm I was home with my husband, before he went to work at 8pm and our little boy tucked up in his cot exhausted by his day out at his Nana's.

Sometime much later in the evening he cried out and when I went to him the sight that greeted me turned me into a gibbering wreck. He had suffered the most horrendous diarrhoea and vomiting I had ever seen possible for such a small person. I wanted to run, I wanted to cry but how could I ?. This was my little boy and for the first time I felt like didn't want him anymore. I was angry with his father for being at work and so therefore it wasn't his problem. I felt like the loneliest person in the world, as far as I was concerned the whole world was asleep, all cosy in their perfect worlds and mine was a singular living nightmare.

My first thoughts were what has he eaten, did I eat any of the same. Will I catch this, and more so how do I start to sort this awful mess out, I couldn't sleep that night and after managing to clean everything I remember laying in bed listening to every snuffle, snort and noise that he made. Amazingly he was totally and blissfully unaware of my feelings towards him and totally unaffected by the entire situation, sadly for me all the wonderment of being a parent ceased from that day on.

*   *   *

Looking back he wasn't a sickly child at all but I must have spent every day for a week or more expecting him to vomit every night, I scrubbed everything with neat bleach, killing all germs, watched what I fed him before he went to bed. I read books and books about the human body and what makes us vomit and what could cause it even memorised the details of how long foods would stay in the stomach. What food digested more quickly than others, and if I can be honest here, I probably reduced my poor little boy's last meal more that I should have just in case he should vomit in the night thus, technically for me controlling the amount of mess I would have to clean up. Of course though he wasn't ill during the night and I gradually relaxed a little and slowly forgot the whole episode. I used to bring up the subject amongst my friends on our mother's meetings and it became apparent that most of them had gone through the same but why oh why did they cope seemingly so easily. How did they even manage to laugh about it?

Funnily enough weeks later I almost used to brag about it just to make me feel that I could cope with anything but underneath I felt confused and very bothered by my mind and the way it could control my entire life when it wanted to.

*   *   *

At 22 years of age to me the good points were I had survived life, having not vomited myself since my teenage years with the food poisoning, had managed a pregnancy and birth without the need to be sick, coped with the one episode of my little boy being ill and felt happy with my lot.

If I take a good look back what had I given up in order to keep my life in order?

A very dull life really, no holidays, no social life as such except maybe a drink at our local club on a Friday night where the average age was 60, but only if my dad was available and happy to babysit for a couple of hours, I only felt secure in my regular environment, in the houses of my friends, my odd shopping routine, but convinced myself that this was what life was all about.

*   *   *

As our toddlers were all around the same age it wasn't long before some the ladies in our group became pregnant with their second child. After a while I too became pregnant, but sadly fell straight back into my habit of asking for the tablets to prevent me from having morning sickness, or rather truthfully for me it was 'just in case' even though once again I was blessed at not being a sufferer at all until my world was to take a knock when on one particular day I did actually feel sickly, I must have been in my 12th or 13th week of my pregnancy and according to all the book technically I should be over the worst. My first instinct was to not eat anything and only sip water. The afternoon progressed to early evening, I had managed to feed my toddler and get him ready for bed before my husband was due home from work as he was back to a day shift. I started to cook his evening meal even though I knew I actually did feel ill. Of course the panic was rising in me but I knew I could fight it and was determined to, but this time my body wanted to fight against me. I took some of my sickness tablets convincing myself that I would be better once they took effect.

*　　*　　*

By the time my husband got home I had turned into a panic stricken maniac, gulping huge breaths of air to fight off the rising waves of nausea, I couldn't bear to go into the kitchen and catch a the aroma of cooked food, so ridiculously I sat in the front garden praying the fresh air would make me feel better. So you can imagine my horror when my body started heaving, as I had only had water all day there was nothing for my stomach to give back except bitter tasting bile, embarrassingly though I couldn't even bear the thought of making it to the downstairs bathroom, as I hated the thought of bending over the toilet bowl. So there I sat on the grass in my own living nightmare and sad to say my husband wasn't helpful or supportive at all.

The following day I still felt very bad and I begged him to stay home from work as I really didn't know how I was going to cope with feeding our toddler, let alone change his dirty nappies, so you can imagine my horror when he refused and told me that he couldn't cope with me if I was going to be ill as he had never ever known me to be ill since the day of my food poisoning 6 years ago and even then he kept out of the way as my parents cared for me. With those words ringing in my ears he left the house, me still in bed and our toddler crying in his cot. What was worse though, was the fact that by now I had started to bleed. Desperately trying not to panic I had no other choice than to literally crawl out of my bed and get to my neighbour begging her for help.

*　　*　　*

While she raced around to my house to collect my now screaming toddler I just sat on her kitchen floor worried about the amount of blood that was now oozing from my body and the sharp pains that were creeping through my abdomen. As soon as she returned she called an ambulance and my husband's place of work, however he insisted that there was nothing he could do and that the doctors would be the only ones to 'sort me out' . . . all I could remember through my fuzziness were the paramedics sticking needles and drips into my arms and my poor darling little boy screaming for me through the letterbox of my neighbours house as I was stretchered into the waiting ambulance and rushed to hospital. Thankfully she also had a little boy around the same age as my son and she assured me that an extra child in the house was not a problem.

*   *   *

I must admit that at the time I didn't have time to think about the chances of me throwing up and it was just as well that I hadn't eaten any food for breakfast as by the time I arrived at the hospital I was bleeding very heavily and the prognosis being that I had lost my baby and was in danger of losing my life if I didn't have surgery. All I could remember was that I did ask the anaesthetist if he could give me something so I wouldn't be sick when I woke up, whether he did or not I don't know but in my head I was reassured.

However what I didn't bargain for was that the poor woman in the bed opposite to me had a terrible reaction to the anaesthetic and spent the best part of the day throwing up into her little cardboard bowls. That alone was enough to put me off of hospitals for good. I prayed that they would pull her curtains around her. I sat with the radio headphones on a full blast in my ears shutting my eyes every time she reached for her little bowl.

I could hardly touch the food that was brought to me at meal times it was just horrible. What I didn't even think to question was my husband's absence. As it was he stayed at home with our young son and it was my parents that came to visit me.

*   *   *

Amazingly many months later I found myself pregnant again and after the elation had settled down I soon got into my routine of asking the Doctor for my regular prescription of anti-sickness pills. I am glad to say that I actually sailed through the following nine months without a hitch and the birth of my second son was very quick, in fact he arrived in less than an hour after arriving at the hospital therefore not even giving me time to consider the fact that I just might be sick during the delivery . . . of course I wasn't and within a couple of days I was back at home, fit and well and a proud mother.

*   *   *

By now most of our circle of mummy's were blessed with two healthy children each and as our oldest children were now all around three years old it was suggested we started attending the local mother and toddler afternoons to prepare them for school. Until now I have to admit that my two children had been very healthy and I hadn't had any more bouts of sickness to deal with. The maddening thing is that if they had a cold I wasn't bothered in the slightest, I could cuddle them when they cried as it was logical to me that they would not be sick from a cold, and I knew that I probably wouldn't catch their coughs and sniffs. So here I was congratulating myself that I was the same as everyone else, and the fact that I was coping with motherhood and all that it entailed until the day whilst at the playgroup that I heard the words "have yours had that tummy bug that's doing the rounds?".

*   *   *

Horrified I wanted to know every detail about who had already been affected, what were the first signs of the illness and most importantly to me had the parents picked up the bug too . . . . I could feel the panic rising in me and all I wanted to do was to leave the toddler group immediately. It was not to be and I had to endure watching in sheer terror as my child was playing with a little friend who just happened to be the one who had been ill only a couple of days previously. I wanted to call him away. I felt an instant hatred towards the mother of the 'infected' child even more so because she was laughing and saying that her younger child would probably start being ill sometime that day but that was just the joys of motherhood. To me she was the devil.

How did she know her younger child would probably be ill? If that was the case, why did she come to the playgroup with a ticking time bomb if that was going to happen I kept on imagining how could she be sure she wasn't breathing horrible germs into the room every time she opened her mouth to speak. I kept going hot and cold, my stomach was churning and the urge to just collect my children together and run home was almost more than I could bear.

Even worse was the weekly routine normally after toddler group we all used to take it in turns to go to one of the houses for a cup of tea and usually a slice of homemade sponge, and it was this woman's germ infested house that we were due to visit that day.

I can remember racking my brains with any excuse not to go and eventually told a lie. Not that I can remember what it was but I know I didn't go to her house that day. The relief when my excuse was accepted was immense and by the time I got home I was a gibbering wreck . . . all I had to do now was to watch and listen for any little sign that either of my children had caught the bug.

So going back to that afternoon, I decided to feed my children their tea early, as far as I was concerned it was a test to see if they were hungry, as I reckoned that if they had contracted the bug then they wouldn't want to eat, and if they did eat anyway by the time they would be ill it would probably be the middle of the night and the

27

food would have digested anyway. As they sat eating I decided to wipe down the pushchair with neat bleach just in case the germs that were so obviously in the room at playgroup were not lurking, therefore putting us in any danger of contamination.

*　　*　　*

Sadly for my children they only had to mention the words 'my tummy hurts' and I would start. I know I used to constantly ask them where the tummy ache was. In my mind, if it was in the chest area of the stomach then I would be convinced it would result in them vomiting. I would methodically get a little bowl for them to use and lay them on the couch with a 'poorly' blanket. I think the hardest of these times were when they were aged from say one year till at least six or seven years of age. It was the not knowing when or if it was actually going to happen which caused me the most distress. I would watch for any little sign that they were about to vomit, any little noise or whimper they made. I would prepare myself.

Once they had actually been sick I felt almost elated that it had happened, hopefully over and done with, I had seemingly coped and now it was just a case of them getting better. To me, it felt that now there couldn't be anything left in their stomach to vomit it was ok. I oddly felt more in control then. I would scrub and bleach everything. The blanket, however clean it still was got put into the washing machine. It was as if I was possessed by some weird compulsive demon that literally took over my body and mind. This feeling however was soon replaced by the agonising thought's that now there was every risk of his brother picking up the same bug or worse me. My first resolution was that I would not eat anything just in case they were ill and I would get it too and secondly I had to decide against feeding my children too much food and what food.

One thing I did do in my evenings was to scour cookery books and read any information on what foods were digested more quickly and what foods stayed in the stomach for the longest amount of time, so I could decide what to feed my children before bedtime knowing that most of it would be digested before they went to sleep. In my head milk didn't count as that was a liquid and probably a saving grace for my children's sake for nutritional purposes.

*   *   *

Ashamedly, by now I also had discovered that Brandy was supposedly administered to patients for medicinal purposes, probably in the old western films on the television, but it was proof enough for me and I now had a little secret bottle hidden away for such occasions, I believed that the strength of the alcohol would kill any germs lurking in my body and eventually that was how I got through the nightmare of it all. Not to get blinding drunk, as I knew I had to be responsible to my family and of course if my husband came home from work and found me in any such state god alone knows what would have happened . . . . all I needed was about an inch or so in a glass of the medicine to stop the panicky feelings and put me in a more relaxed state of mind. It was the only way I could cope and sadly only I knew about my very guilty secret.

As for not eating I used to cook the evening meal for my husband and tell him I had eaten with the children. He had no reason to doubt me and never did.

Of course we all survived and I can't even remember if we contracted 'the bug'. I am sure we didn't. So after a week or so of excuses not to visit friend's house's therefore excluding us from any outings even a trip to the shops, I gradually fell back into my routine and the panic was again forgotten. It was odd that when I did indeed get through and in my head cope as a normal parent I used to feel happy inside but, had I been truthful with myself turning to and living just on a glass of brandy here and there and also by now as an extra reassurance a regular spoonful of Kaolin and Morphine (just in case) I would and should have known that I was only masking my nightmares.

*   *   *

Children's birthday parties were another hurdle I had to try and cross. As a child I used to go to parties held by friends but there was always a child that would overeat and end up being sick. It took the fun out of the day and I usually just wanted to go home. My own children always used to ask for a party but I would be a little hesitant, mainly as I hated the thought having to deal with the possibility that a child would over eat and vomit in my home. Oddly my youngest child used to get so over excited he would make himself ill and would spend his birthday in bed whilst his friends had the party anyway. Gradually I just stopped having parties for them and as you will later discover due to our circumstances it wasn't always appropriate to have a party at home

*   *   *

The day my husband came home from work early as he was ill was something I didn't ever want to happen. He hadn't mentioned that a few of his work mates had all suffered a bout of sickness and diarrhoea and unfortunately my husband had now seemed to have contracted this bug.

As soon as he came in the door and told me I immediately went into the utmost state of panic imaginable. The first things that went through my head were a calculation of how long he could have been harbouring this germ, and had he had much contact with the children. I was desperate to get him away from me and the children and can remember making him go to bed. The next was to get out the bleach and wash down where he had touched since being home as well as thoroughly cover the toilet and sink in neat bleach, how the skin on my hands didn't fall off I just don't know. Next was to pour a glass of Brandy to calm me down and convince myself that it would protect me.

The children would be limited on their food for that teatime as I could not cope if they too were ill, and there was no way I was going to sleep in the same room as my husband as I didn't want him to breathe any germs any-where near me. Just taking him a glass of water I held my breath as I entered the room and shouted from the other side of the door to find out if he needed anything. I know this all must read as being totally ridiculous but believe me it's as if your body and mind just wants to shut down and make everything just go away. The feeling of wanting to curl up in a ball and cry and just wishing to be alone was awful.

We always seemed to get through these times and when life was considerably back to normal I had this weird feeling of wanting to tell everyone that we had been affected by the latest bug, not only that be almost proud that I had deemed myself as able to cope, but at what cost to my poor children and husband. I don't to this day know why I used to do that.

*   *   *

Not that it has any bearing on my problems or phobia but my marriage to this person sadly ended by the time my boys were aged around 3 and 5 years respectively and I found myself back living in one room at my parents house, the boys in bunk-beds and me in a double bed. Space was tight and I always will be eternally grateful to my parents for taking me back home under the very stressful situation that led to the divorce.

Being back within the bosom of my family I felt a little more relaxed as I felt as if I had the support of my parents and mentally it wasn't just up to me to take care of the children if they were ill. I had to get myself back to work part time as I had no financial support whatsoever from their father and I was lucky enough that my father would sometimes be able to babysit as he had days off during the week as opposed to the weekend. I was able to return part time to the bank.

*   *   *

The oldest child was now at school and life was actually not too bad. I can remember having to go to my first parents evening and even though I wanted to see my son's school work I found I didn't want to touch anything in the classroom. I tried to avoid sitting on a child's chair and didn't want to handle my child's schoolbooks as I was convinced that there was certain to be bugs and germs lurking in every corner of that room. I was just so desperate to get out and be able to wash my hands and change my clothes to rid me of any risk of contamination.

When my son started to have his cookery lessons at school I used to be repulsed at the thought of having to eat what he proudly brought home. I somehow used to pretend to eat the piece of cake and when he was convinced I had eaten some I would hide it in a pocket until I could throw it into the rubbish bin. How I hated myself for deceiving him, I hope he was never aware.

*   *   *

Another issue that I feel very guilty about is that when my children used to bring home the letter regarding the school outing. On the bottom of the letter there was always the tear off strip asking for any mum's that would come along on the trip to supervise the children. My son's always used to ask me if I would be a helper, and as much as I wished I could say yes there was absolutely no way on this earth that I could have done it. Just the thought of getting on the coach was enough to give me palpitations but the thought of being saddled with a travel sick child was impossible for me to even contemplate. I used to wait at the school gate to wave the excited children off on their trip to where ever and at the same time watch so enviously at the mum's that were going on the trip all clutching buckets lined with carrier bags for the unfortunate children, but all so happy and excited just like the children. My morbid fascination oddly enough, was to be there at the school gates for when the coach returned back so I would see how many buckets had been used, relined and how big the bag was that contained the used bags . . . . why was that ??? . . . . I would grill my poor children asking how many of the children on the trip were sick however one thing I must mention here is that I would unknowingly to my children dose them with medication telling them that the tablets were to make them strong for their day out.

*   *   *

I actually enjoyed being back at work even though it was only part time. I had a friend who was a trained nurse and she also had children around the same ages as my two sons. In fact our eldest sons went to school together and she used to child-mind for a few friends including me. I was quite happy for my toddler to go to her house as she was fastidious in her cleaning regime and food preparation.

It was during this time when I had returned to working in the bank that one of my work colleagues was diagnosed with cancer. She had several treatments of chemotherapy which obviously made her very poorly. Our friends and colleagues in the bank used to take turns to visit her to keep her spirits up and even now I am ashamed to say that every time they asked me to visit her I always had an excuse ready as I physically couldn't make myself go to the hospital as I imagined that she would possibly vomit when I was visiting, and if it wasn't her then surely another of the patients would. I used to bombard my friends with questions about their visits and how many people were on her ward and if they were all sickly. Even when she was sent home to recuperate I continued to make excuses not to visit always scared that she would vomit in my company. Sadly she passed away at the young age of 26 years old. I hated myself so much for being such a selfish coward. Her funeral was heartbreaking and I wept buckets, of course they were for the loss of a dear friend, but also I cried for myself and what a horrible uncaring person I must have appeared to be. I just wished I could tell someone why I didn't visit, as much as I wanted to, but I knew that no-one would understand me.

*   *   *

Sadly I didn't learn my lesson as only a few months later, yet another female friend was diagnosed, however this time it was even more poignant as we both used to be at school together and both had children around the same ages of 3 and 5 years old. . . . . How did I deal with it ? . . . . I more or less turned my back on her, I couldn't help it, I thought about going to visit her many times but I was scared firstly that she would be ill when I visited and secondly that she might ask me to care for her children for a day or so. The thought of being responsible for two extra children as well as my own two was a nightmare not even worth considering. Tragically she too passed away and I still carry the guilt that I could have done so much to help her family but again to them I probably looked as if I didn't care and awful as it sounds, they never spoke to me again.

*   *   *

It was while I was working I was to meet another man, he was a customer at my place of work and he happened to ask me out for a lunch one day. All seemed pretty harmless and we got on well. He would occasionally take me and the boys out on a Sunday. Within a year we had bought a little house and planned a holiday in Cornwall, all sounds lovely until I suddenly got panic attacks of the children being carsick. Up until now I hadn't really gone very far distances with the children in the car. I do recall one time when the youngest was about 10 months old and was sick in the car once and so had avoided long journeys at all costs.

So now I had to think of a plan as to how to survive the long journey of at least seven hours. I knew of a medicine that could be given to children to help them sleep, although I am not sure if it is available now, but anyway I had purchased a bottle of this stuff as I used to dose my children regularly with this medicine if I was aware of any school illnesses . . . . why did I give it to them ?? . . . . Well in my head if they were in a deeper sleep maybe they wouldn't wake up and be ill. I know this all must make me look like a terrible mother but it was all about peace of mind.

Now this medicine also claimed to be effective against travel sickness if administered the previous evening before the day of travel. I still couldn't bring myself to think about spending all those hours in the car and eventually came up with a genius plan of travelling through the night, making out that it would be a lot better as the children could sleep in the back of the car if we put the seats down and made it an adventure, amazingly I convinced my partner to agree, as they weren't his children I made out they would be a nightmare in the car during the day, and if we left home around midnight we would miss all the traffic, they would sleep and we would be in Cornwall on the Saturday morning thus making the most of our every holiday minute. I didn't consider the fact that my partner had done a full day's work and would be doing the driving, it was all about being able to dose the poor things up with the medicine and pray they slept all the way.

We had a lovely holiday as I can recall but the maddening thing was that I couldn't control the return journey as well and was forced to endure the drive back during the day. I know I dosed up the children well and truly and we actually did make it back all in one piece, another hurdle for me seemingly jumped over or so I thought.

*   *   *

In time it became sadly obvious that this partner was an alcoholic of the very secret kind, amazingly he managed to keep it a secret from me probably because of the children and the fact that they spent every weekend with their father. He was clever enough not to give anything away so that they would tell their dad. It was on such a weekend when the boys were away that he tried to explain to me his reason for liking a drink and how he came from a background of 'pub life'.His parents were publicans for many years and it was a way of life, probably the only way of life that he knew. I found that a little amusing and a sad excuse as I can recall my mother telling me stories of how her Aunt and Uncle were publicans in Winchester and how she used to be in the bar on the counter top at a very young age, and there is no way my mother's family harboured any secret alcoholics, a G and T now and then of course, just not the whole bl**dy bottle though.

*   *   *

Anyway going back to the weekends when the boys would visit their father. Oh how I loved those weekends, not for the romantic sense though, more selfishly I could relax, have no worrying thought when I went to bed that I would be woken in the night by one of them stumbling around saying they didn't feel well . . . I used to hate it when one of them would call out 'mummy I've got a hot tummy'. Now a 'hot tummy' always used to be a sick tummy. I hate myself for admitting this dear reader but I lived for my child free weekends, I was glad to be away from them, purely for that reason alone.

*   *   *

It was on such a weekend that we had agreed to hold a party at our house, not for any particular reason, just a get together for a few friends that we had made, most of whom, didn't have children. I can clearly remember having to work on that Saturday morning and arranged to meet my partner by the supermarket to finish off the required party food shopping. As soon as I met him I could tell he had been drinking and was horrified when he told me he was going to stop in the pub till closing time and would be home in time to help with the preparation. Easy said and done as we both had our own cars and had driven separately to the town on that morning.

By the time he arrived at the house late afternoon he was almost unable to walk, how the hell he drove the 15 miles home I still don't know to this day. All I can recall is that my panic overtook my reasoning and all I could think of is that drunken people usually vomit. I went into a total frenzy screaming and shouting at him while he crawled around the lounge on his knees belching and farting disgustingly and uncontrollably.

I cancelled the party he managed to pack a case and walked or rather stumbled out of my life going back to live in his mother's house. So here I was once again back to just me and the children and my continuing living nightmare of having to cope alone, but relieved that |I didn't have to endure the added horror of a drunken partner around my children.

*   *   *

It was around about this time that my eldest son who must have been about 8 years old by now began to suffer very bad bouts on tonsillitis. I could deal with this even though he would sometimes vomit due to a high temperature during his very poorly days. As I reasoned with myself that when he did vomit it was not because of a bug and just his temperature I was at least able to help him even though sadly it was still at arm's length and with a glass of Brandy for me.

Eventually the doctors decided that his tonsils would have to be removed. At the time I was pleased for him to be free of this awful situation having been a sufferer in my younger days, until it came to the day of his operation.

As much as I tried to convince myself to take him to the hospital I just couldn't do it and I will always be eternally grateful that my father happened to have a day off and so using the excuse that I couldn't get time off work he took him for me. The same came to the evening when he could be visited. All I could think of was that not so much if he was sick after the operation but more so what if the other patients on his ward were also liable to be sick.

I am not too sure what excuse I made but, bless them, my darling parents went to visit him and reported back that he was well and could come home the following day. I am glad to say that when he was home I could deal with him and his sore throat.

*   *   *

Now you must be wondering by this stage why I didn't get professional help . . . I did actually get so desperate with life that I did go to my doctor and try to explain my dilemma. Maybe I didn't come across as strong as I should have but I can recall the conversation.

Me. "Please can you help me I hate it when people are sick and I don't want to catch any virus they may be carrying and be sick myself."

Dr.(frowning)... "We are sick for different reasons it's nature's way of safe guarding our body it's natural and not always infectious"

End of conversation . . . . I felt stupid, let down and still as desperate especially as it had taken all of my utmost inner strength to open up and confide in my doctor.

However I did find an article or more an advert in the surgery for an expert in dealing with phobia's and soul destroying situations, marriage guidance in-fact everything life could possibly throw at you. I attended a short interview prior my first session where the councillor asked a few questions to build a picture of me and my situation.

I explained how I was living alone with my 2 children as the ex partner turned out to be alcohol dependant and how that alone turned me into a jabbering lunatic on top of trying to deal with my phobia which had engulfed me since the age of eight years old. I explained my fear of vomiting. Not only if it concerned me and my children but in strangers, how I couldn't even walk past an obvious patch on the pavement.

She very gently took my hand and told me she could help and proceeded to tell me how she would deal with my fears. So you can imagine my total horror when she uttered the words "to learn to deal with our fears we have to face them head on and prove they will not harm us". She went on to explain how I would start by looking at pictures of vomit and of people vomiting, then progress to films of the same. Just by listening to her telling me this my 'flight of fear' mode took over I went from hot to cold, my heart hammering inside my body, I felt sick and lightheaded and promised myself that I would not be coming back . . . and I stayed true to myself and never kept my next appointment. I knew then this was going to be a life-long battle and I would try to make myself better on my own terms.

*　　*　　*

So going back to the partner who liked his drink too much . . . . He came back after 6 months and promised me he was a new person and didn't need to drink. He was at the time full of remorse and felt maybe we should make a fresh start he even suggested we consider having a baby of our own, he promised me the world, sent me flowers and generally went well over the top. Surprisingly he took all the blame and thankfully for me I didn't have to explain my phobia to him . . . . it was still very much my secret demon.

During the 6 months apart my partner had lost his driving licence for a drink/driving offence. So now it was up to me to drive us everywhere. More stress for me as I had to juggle the school run, be able to drive us both to work, which often meant that I had to do the journey twice as I worked part time and my partner full time. He did use public transport on some occasions, but, in time the whole situation began to tell on the family.

*   *   *

It was during these days that my oldest son, he must have been about ten years old by now, had started to ask about going to live with his father. To any outsider a mother that would give up her child so easily would be considered a terrible person. I on the other hand did not put up much resistance. All I could think of was that I would be free from the responsibility. It would be so much better for me as I would only have one child to deal with when it came to any school bugs, shockingly I couldn't wait for him to go. What I didn't do was to get to the root of the problem and why he wanted to go and live with his dad. I don't really know what my son's used to think of me. I hardly ever used to cuddle or kiss them or show any real affection, I wouldn't even let them breathe over me if I could help it. I more or less raised them at arm's length. I often wonder now if they ever noticed the way that I was towards them. What I didn't bargain for though, was the massive effect this situation was going to have on my youngest son. He missed his older brother very much as now they only spent the weekends together. One weekend was spent at my home and the following at their father's home. Now you would think that I would have missed having my own son around me, but no, I dreaded the weekends when it was my turn to have them both. I spent the whole weekend worrying if he may have carried a bug from his school to our home and was relieved once I had endured the weekend without any illness and he was back with his father.

*   *   *

I didn't get a lot of input from my partner when it came to my children. He didn't seem curious when I allowed my son to move back to his father's house. Personally I don't think he cared that much for them anyway. Life just carried on, it was a horrible part of my life really, I felt trapped by this powerful, soul destroying 'thing' that governed my every waking moment of every day of my life, and yet I could still not bring myself to admit to anyone how I felt. On many occasions I used to dream and wish for the days when the boys would be grown up and not living at home any more. What sort of mother ever wishes that for her children ?. . . . Please don't judge me to be a bad person, I

39

loved my children but at the same time I felt as if it was all too much especially when they were ill. That part of it I hated.

*   *   *

So you can imagine my shock when my partner decided that we needed a change to our lifestyle and announced that he had been in touch with a company that could give us our own business to run . . . . He had signed us up to run our own pub !!!!!

He assured me that as a landlord he would not drink as he had to be in control of any situation and a drunken landlord is a bad landlord. He made it all sound so wonderful, being able to live in the same place as we worked, the children would have me all the time, even though the oldest had by now moved in with his father. No more child minders and being pushed off to friends houses if I was working in the school holidays, I will be honest he did paint a very good picture and a few months later in June 1988 we moved into our picturesque village pub. I found the time to study catering and hospitality and a fresh start had begun.

*   *   *

Now you wouldn't believe that a catering and hospitality course would have such an effect on my life. The more I learned about food and what could make you ill the more it fed my phobia. Things like rice for example. Did you know that if you are ill after eating a Chinese meal the most likely candidate for the food poisoning is the rice. Cooked rice which is not stored properly or not re-heated to the required temperature can make you very ill. Although I loved the cooking side to my coursework the more I learned about the problems that food can create I vowed I would never put myself in any knowing danger and would probably never eat our again. My lucky excuse was that I had a pub/restaurant to run so wouldn't need to anyway. The good thing that came of this was that I was fastidious in my own food storing and preparation and was proud that I created a very busy little eatery, confident that my food was good and cooked properly.

*   *   *

So all looks wonderful in my world doesn't it ? . . . Wrong, I hadn't bargained for the rowdy drunks on a Friday and Saturday night coming in and spending all their wages on beer then usually throwing it all back up across the car-park on their way home. I would refuse to look outside in the mornings and used to make my partner go outside to hose down the entire outside. He wanted the pub so he could clean up the mess.

It got worse though as it was up to me to clean the inside of the pub which naturally included the ladies and gents toilets. I used to hate waking up every morning wondering what sort of state they would be in, If I Look back now there actually weren't many times that the ladies were ever left in a mess, but the men's were a different story. I hated having to clean the men's toilet. I used to hold my breath and screw my eyes up just peeping at a small section of the room at any one time. It was a huge relief when I could see that no-one had vomited in the urinal or the toilet. Sometimes in the evenings when I felt more confident after a couple of glasses of wine I used to ask the regular male customers why they had to drink to the point of being sick. Many of them told me that it was sometimes just the smell of their own urine that made them sick. They didn't feel ill it was just a reaction. In an odd way I accepted that explanation as I then knew that it was not a 'bug' type of sickness therefore it wasn't anything that I was likely to catch.

Eventually, with a lot of persuasion, pleading and begging but ashamed of explaining the truth of the matter I was relieved when we were able to employ a cleaner even though it was a costly and cowardly way out. Looking back we probably couldn't afford one but at the time I didn't really care, it took care of the situation and I quite happily stayed in the kitchen cooking, oblivious to the goings on in the bar.

*   *   *

Around the same time that we took over the running of the pub my father had retired and was in need of a hobby or something to do as my mother was still working full time. So, he used to come over for a lunchtime session and run the bar while I cooked and served the lunches. This seemed to work very well but the situation altered when my partner decided that he would be 'off duty' for the lunchtime and gradually he started to drink on these 'off duty' times. To spare any bad feelings as it is over 23 years ago now, all I will say is that within 6 months of starting 'afresh' we were over £12,000 in debt and he was drinking over 30 PINTS a day. I know this as I got my father and a friend to count for me one day . . . . He got so bad one night that he lost control, verbally abused the customers that we had, smashed all the windows and doors and once again walked out of my life leaving me with the consequences. I never saw him again after that and only a couple of years ago I learned he had died aged just 51.

So there I was with a pub to run, the children aged just 9 and 12 years old, tormented by the fact they had been separated. Massive debts of which I was totally unaware of as 'he' used to 'do the books', at least I didn't have any time to give my phobia much attention, I had to get on with life in order for us to all survive. What a great start to 1989.

* * *

The cleaner stayed and used to serve behind the bar in the evenings as well as my father who still helping during the day, it was amazing how the customers all rallied to help. One man in particular just stepped in and took over, not only the pub but eventually my life too. We kept the place going and slowly repaired the physical and financial damage. We eventually became a couple and to make extra money this particular person found work outside of the pub to make life a little easier, my dad still did the lunchtime sessions and slowly we managed to reduce the massive debt I had been left with.

What I didn't bargain for though, having been told by doctors that it would be very unlikely I would be able to conceive after my many gynaecological operations was to suddenly find myself pregnant at the age of 32 years old.

* * *

Incredibly all my anxieties returned with a massive force. Here I was once again pleading with my doctor to give me medication for morning sickness, my excuse this time was that I had a business to run and could not afford to be ill at all. I hated the thought of being pregnant but had to be very careful of what I said or indicated as my partner as he was now sadly had lost a child through a cot death, a little boy. At first his reactions were of shock and almost horror. He was convinced that this baby would also die at a young age and therefore I was struggling to keep my emotions in check and pretend everything was wonderful but at the same time I had to deal with the very difficult reactions from my partner. I remember he got very drunk one night and he told me he didn't need the worry or the bother of a baby or me. It was hard to deal with at the time and yet I had his parents elated that there was a new baby on the horizon and perhaps it would bring a sort of closure to the agony that the cot death had bestowed upon the family.

I was angry having got through what I felt were the worst times with my children and the childhood illnesses and how I dealt with their sickness problems, to suddenly have the realisation that I was going to have to start all over again.

The only saving grace was that as I got nearer to my due date I was excluded from all involvement of the business. If we were really busy with food I would help in the kitchen but I was happy to spend my evenings upstairs out of the way. Not having to watch customers getting drunk then spend every second compulsively watching their every move, even down to how long they spent in the gents toilets, with me wondering if they were throwing up the copious amounts of beer they had consumed.

*   *   *

The birth of my third son was very uneventful and I was back cooking at the pub within a few days. As we were normally very busy at the weekends my In-laws were very good at taking the baby for the entire weekend which was a bonus for me not having to worry about him, although it was difficult when it was my turn to have my eldest son at home for the weekend but in fairness I had to try and keep some sort of normality in their lives.

By the time the baby was five months old we had decided it was best for everyone if we sold the business and tried to live a more conventional life. What I didn't bargain for, was that just two weeks after we moved out of the pub and into our new house that my partner and father of the baby was to suffer the most horrendous motorcycle accident on his way to work which left him very badly injured.

*   *   *

Now this may sound ridiculous but I used to and still do like to watch the hospital documentaries and also the hospital drama's just out of interest to see how many people were sick as in throw up sick, you see I felt in control of the situation in as much that I could always turn off the television if I didn't like what I was watching. Well this was to be a very small turning point in my self help process and I finally managed to watch a whole episode of casualty (where someone throws up every week) as I knew they were only acting and it was a mouthful of vegetable soup that was just spat out. It was a start and a revelation for me in a sad sort of way. Maybe it was this that got me through the next couple of weeks.

*   *   *

As I raced to the hospital with my young baby I didn't know what to expect and for probably the only time in my life I went into the emergency area without even a thought of who else may be there, and what if they were vomiting. It was a very worrying time in our life and the daily trips to the hospital were difficult as he was in a large ward and naturally there were patients who did react to their operations, mainly vomiting afterwards. I used to scan the ward as soon as I approached it making a check for those that had the tell-tale cardboard bowls balanced carefully on their pillows ready for use. I think I spent each visit watching intently these patients praying they would stay sleeping till my nightmare of visiting time was over.

It was a common rule that only two visitors were allowed at the bedside and so if any other family members came to visit I couldn't wait to get out of the ward assuring them they could stay as long as they wanted. I was just relieved to be away from the environment. Eventually my partner was released from hospital but his injuries were so bad that he was left unable to work for the following two and a half years.

*   *   *

Within a few of months after the accident and having sold everything we owned to buy food for us plus nappies and other essentials for the baby we were left with no other choice than to hand back the keys of our house to the estate agents. Cancel our mortgage and move back to my partner's parent's home.

We were in a desperate situation and as they could only offer just one room for us so it was decided that my middle son who was by now almost ten years old would have to go and live with his father. As awful as it sounds and I cry as I write it, for me it was a relief that I was once again freed of the nightmare of having a child of school age to cope with, should he be infected with a school sickness bug . . . . you, as a reader will have no idea how this horror consumed my every living day to the point that I can't recall ever enjoying my children and celebrating their lives.

*   *   *

So by now it is 1990. I have two children living with their father, a temporarily disabled partner and a 9 month old baby. No home of our own, hardly any possessions having had to sell them all. Living in one room, sharing a house with not only my partner's parent's but his ageing grandfather and unknown to me at the time his alcoholic uncle who had been badly treated by a woman in his youth and from then on had spent his life working and drinking his way through every day intent on never getting married or involved with women again. We were very grateful we had a roof over our heads but it wasn't easy.

Amazingly I did cope with nursing my partner slowly back to normal as it didn't involve him actually being ill and risking him vomiting and the 'in-laws' doted on the baby and so every minute of their free time was taken with him. What I hated most of all was the uncle and the state he used to get into.

He would stumble about the place belching and slurring his words and worst of all it was a house rule that we all had to sit down at the dining table together for our evening meal. Unfortunately the uncle would finish work early in the afternoon and then spend the hours till our meal time either at the local pub or drinking in his bedroom. To have to endure those mealtimes watching as he tried to get some food into his mouth used to make me feel so physically ill I could hardly eat my food.

*   *   *

The weekends were even worse as he would get so drunk sometimes that he would vomit. The arguments that would then erupt between my partner's mum (as it was her brother) and her husband were awful. She used to be the one to have to clean his bedding and wash down the bedroom walls where he had projectile vomited.

I used to lie in bed at night listening and waiting for him to stumble his way past our bedroom door on route to the bathroom or his bedroom. I could hardly bare to go into the bathroom first thing in the morning for fear of what state he may have left it in. There was another toilet downstairs in the utility room which I could use but sometimes he had got to that one first before crawling his way up the stairs. At this point I think I must have reached rock bottom. I hated every single day of my life and used to pray for a way out.

*   *   *

My In-laws were very concerned as to the possibilities of my partner ever being able to work properly again and be able to support our family unit, so they discussed the option of us maybe moving to France with them and opening a restaurant as I had my catering experience and we both had the expertise of running a public house. It was decided that we would drive over in two vehicles and tow a caravan as well. My middle son was to travel with us as well as the baby who was by now about fourteen months old.

We scoured the papers for businesses for sale and made many plans for our chosen area to visit and excitedly we booked tickets for the ferry.

*   *   *

Ok time for a husband funny

Before I tell you about our journey here is my husband's tale of his ferry boat crossing when he was on a trip to the Hook of Holland. He was part of the under 15's England basket Ball Team and they were all travelling by ferry for a very important match and all dressed in their smart trousers and blazers. Unfortunately the crossing was a very rough one and four of the lads did not travel too well . . . . he tried to picture the scene of these big strapping lads all with long hair... going back to the beginning of the 1980's when the mullet hair style was in fashion, all sat by the windows in their chairs, all had been sick against the windows and were now asleep with their hair stuck to the windows with the offending mess. When they eventually stood up to disembark they looked frightful with their hair sticking up at all angles and certainly not the trendy sports hero's they started out to be, but, as he said it was funny in a funny sort of way especially for a bunch of fifteen year olds.

*   *   *

Sat waiting at the dockside to board the ferry I couldn't believe how well I was coping. I had taken a couple of travel sickness pills and insisted that my two sons take them as well. Eventually we were on board the ship. I felt slightly panicky as more and more people got on board but promised myself I would stay outside on the top deck for the whole six hour journey and not be trapped inside. As soon as we set sail I asked my partner for a large glass of brandy with the excuse we may as well start off the holiday with a treat. It did the trick and took the edge off of my nerves.

It was a fairly calm journey but my partner's mother suffered very badly. I just kept well away from her and kept focussed on my two children who were amazing throughout the entire six hour journey. My confidence in my children helped me so much and we finally arrived in France looking forward to our adventure.

*   *   *

A whole week was spent driving around viewing properties, and not on any one day did I have to cope with any sickness. I was very careful what I fed the children. I had taken a big supply of baby food in jars for the baby. Otherwise we had a boring diet of mainly French bread, cheese and salads. My confidence grew a little every day and I actually enjoyed the fact that I was actually coping with every single day. For me it was a revelation in itself.

*   *   *

All too soon it was time to travel back to the UK and we made our way back to St. Malo to catch our ferry. The nearer we got to the port the darker the sky was getting and the trees were starting to sway quite violently. All I could think about was how rough was the sea going to be and after a wonderful week my fears all started tumbling around in my head. My mouth kept going dry, my heart pounding and all I could think about was how many people would be sea-sick. I had the travel sickness pills and once again took a couple and dosed both the children. My partner didn't want any and as his parent's were in their own vehicle they weren't given the opportunity to be offered the choice.

By the time we were waiting to board it was obvious the weather was fast closing in and I prayed that the trip would be cancelled. For me it was a case of No such luck!!

Slowly one by one the cars all filed onto the ferry which by now was rocking pretty badly. It had started to rain and we all shuffled up the stairs from the parking deck to the lounges. I was desperate for a glass of brandy to calm me but the bar was not permitted to open until the ship had set sail.

Before long we were underway and the moment the ship left the relative safety of the harbour it was apparent we were in for a horrendous journey home. I was amazed at the amount of people that had already eaten from the cafe on board as I couldn't or wouldn't eat anything just in case I was sea sick, all I wanted was brandy, which eventually my partner went off to get for me after I practically begged him to do. He sensed I was almost in tears of desperation.

*   *   *

About an hour into the journey the bar was suddenly closed and a warning message played over the public address system forbidding anyone to venture outside onto the decks as the seas were getting progressively worse and we were heading straight into a force ten gale.

At this point my partner's mother was vomiting into her sick bags that she had been given by the staff on board the ship. I was mortified as I watched person after person take these bags. I was desperate to get away, the feeling of panic rising in me to uncontrollable proportions. I was sweating, going hot and cold, was desperate for another brandy but the bars were all closed and worse to happen my baby vomited all over himself and his pushchair.

If I could have thrown myself off the ship at the time I think I would have done and even now as I type this I can still feel the panic in me. This must and has been up until then my worst ever nightmare of a situation. Thankfully I think my partner sensed I was in a desperate situation and thank god he took the baby to the gents toilets to clean him up and what did I do ??? . . . . I took my other son by the hand and as quickly as I could and against the rules I took him outside onto the deck.

Everywhere I looked people were vomiting over the floor, over the side of the ship, I was in a total state of uncontrollable panic and acting most probably very erratically. I just kept a firm hold of my son and kept walking on the deck, getting soaking wet but I didn't care. I don't even recall what was going through my mind I just could not comprehend going back into the lounge so I kept going kept walking aimlessly until by a pure stroke of luck I found a small area under a stairway where about six other people were sheltering. It seemed that they were the only ones out of all the passengers on the journey that had not been taken ill and that is where we stayed safe in their little group and endured the journey home.

By the time we had docked we all looked frightful. The salt water had plastered our hair to our faces and having to walk through the lounge back to the car park area was awful. There were vomit bags strewn everywhere, the rubbish bins overflowing and passengers were still being sick even though we had docked. Our car journey home took forever as we had to keep stopping for my partner's mother to continually throw up. She took several days to recuperate and I vowed never to step on board a ship ever again.

*   *   *

As it was our plans to move to France didn't materialise due to many reasons so we had no options but to stay living with my partner's parents and hope that eventually our life would take a turn for the better. Slowly and surely day by day my partner got stronger and eventually returned to work. However it had taken us three years since his accident before we were in a position to be able to once again afford our own home.

The day we finally moved into our own home was such a massive relief for me. I was free of having to endure the daily nightmare of living in the same house as the alcoholic uncle. I had my own bathroom which only we used, I was elated and our life settled into some normality. I coped with the weekend visits from my two sons and eventually the middle one returned to living with us.

I am not sure whether it was at this point but I feel perhaps having had to endure such a host of emotions looking back perhaps mentally I was a getting a little stronger.

*   *   *

By now my youngest child has just started school so I felt perhaps it was time for me to try to get a sense of purpose in my life and try to move forward so I applied for the job as a kitchen manager in the same school that my son was attending and actually got the job.

As I mentioned earlier in the book it felt odd doing a job around children and the school aspect of 'sickness bugs' that were seemingly easily transmitted, but I wonder now if subconsciously I was trying to confront my fear but under my terms and not those of a councillor. I knew I had everything under control and therefore I could push the boundaries.

At first when I started the job I would only stay in the huge kitchen as I had no reason to enter the dining hall or any part of the school. One of the rules of the catering company was that, if any member of my staff, as food handlers were ill they were not to come to school until they were completely recovered. So my kitchen was to me a bug free zone. We used boiling water to sterilise all the cooking pots, dinner plates and utensils. I was meticulous in my hygiene routine at all times.

If any child happened to be taken ill during the lunch time huge precautions were taken not to bring any of the affected plates or cutlery into the kitchen. It was normally disposed of, but I must say usually the child was taken to the sick room before they had a chance to vomit.

Gradually though and much to the delight of my young son who was proud to boast that his mummy was the cook I started to make myself enter the dining hall to collect the used plates ready for washing. This in itself was a massive achievement for me and perhaps a step in the right direction.

Next it was to walk the corridor past the school sick room to the staff room and make myself take the lunchtime rolls for the teaching staff if they were unusually busy. I felt compelled to have a look to see if there was a sick child in the room, and finally began to realise it didn't happen very often and that most of it was in my head. For the first time in years I felt just ever so slightly proud of myself.

* * *

As the months passed we became financially more secure and eventually bought ourselves a little pleasure boat to use on our local canal. It was the most amazing fun I had had with all of my children in years. Life was getting better for us as a family. My parents fell in love with our little boat and the excitement of it all and they too soon had a boat of their own. We had some lovely happy times spending entire weekends on the water as a family unit. Life was finally on the up. I had a job which I loved, my partner was working and I started enjoying the fact I was a mother I could relax a little but I always had a bottle of brandy in the house as well as a variety of medications for sickness and upset stomachs in my bathroom cabinet.

So it was a bit of a shock when all was fantastic in my life that my partner came home from work feeling ill. He had a very bad headache and felt very sick. I immediately felt panic rising in me but determined to stay calm I poured my glass of brandy and insisted he took a plastic bowl with him and went to bed to minimise the risk of him breathing any germs around the kitchen and lounge area before the children returned home from school.

Unfortunately for him my partner became worse and worse and was becoming so anxious that I eventually had to go to him. He couldn't see properly and needed his vomit bowl cleaning out. Taking a huge gulp of air I managed to clean the bowl for him and called a doctor. I forbid the children to come upstairs as they had now returned from school and wanted feeding. I racked my brains of what to give them in case they caught the illness and gave them a small amount of food to keep them happy. The doctor arrived and diagnosed meningitis and called an ambulance immediately.

*   *   *

Unaware of the severity of the situation I phone my parents and asked if they could come and look after my children whilst I went to the hospital. The paramedics arrived and took my partner away. By the time I had organised everything at home and made my way to the hospital by car it was over an hour since I had last seen him. When I arrived I was shocked to see that he had been put into an isolation ward. The doctors came to see me and said that until they had a confirmed diagnosis as to whether it was viral or bacterial meningitis he would remain isolated. All of this time I didn't even consider where he had caught the bug from and it was only when the doctors advised me to keep a close watch on my children and if I felt ill in any way, that I was to contact the hospital immediately, did the reality of the situation sink in. I went home in a state of shock, panic and dread. The first thing I did was to strip the bed and wash all the covers. The house was cleaned with a solution of bleach. I was determined to eradicate and germs that could be lurking in our home. There absolutely no way I was going to allow anyone of us be ill. I drank a lot of brandy that evening.

*   *   *

The following day I telephoned the hospital for an update and the doctors informed me it was a viral form and he was not in any danger. I asked him the possibilities of me or my children being affected and he confirmed it would be highly unlikely but just to be aware. I felt like I was living on a knife edge. Every cough or sneeze from my children I would immediately get that horrible panicky, hot and cold sensation shoot through my body. I could hardly eat for fear of me getting ill. I couldn't sleep, but would lay in bed almost waiting for one of the children to call out but very thankfully within a week life was getting back to normal. My husband had been released from the hospital and fortunately for me and my children we were all spared the illness. It was a big reality wake up call for me though. To have survived a situation as severe as this, was proof that just perhaps I could cope as long as everything was meticulously cleaned and bleached and I could maintain a germ free home.

*   *   *

A couple of years later he fell ill again only this time he had the misfortune to suffer appendicitis. It was again a tricky situation as we had actually been out for something to eat with my partner's parents and he became ill during the evening. My first thoughts were that he had eaten something that didn't agree with him or the food was bad and I immediately recalled how I felt when I had food poisoning all those years ago. I kept questioning him as to where his pain was. He just kept saying it was almost in his groin. I managed to get him home, a nightmare for me as we had to make several stops for him to be sick. By the time we got home I decided to call the doctor. Describing his symptoms and telling the doctor we had been out at a restaurant he confirmed food poisoning. The bad point of this was that I had a feeling that he was suffering from something else. I sat with him all night, he was in agony. I sought comfort in a large glass of brandy. Incredibly though this time I was able to cope with him vomiting I felt so sorry for him. By the morning he was very ill and I called the paramedics. Thankfully they arrived just in time and by the time they got him to the operating theatre his appendix had ruptured. I had been thoroughly tested by my fear of vomiting but I had once again survived. This was a massive breakthrough for me. I finally realised that I could care for my nearest and dearest if they were sick. BUT and it is a very big BUT only if the cause of vomiting was not due to any contagious bug that I would contract.

*   *   *

It had been a long painful process after my partner's road accident and after several years of fighting with insurance companies and several visits to solicitors he was award a fair sum of money. His first words were to me that we should get married having been together for many years and then celebrate with a well deserved a holiday abroad.

As he uttered the words instead of jumping for joy and being excited, I felt the panicky, heart thumping sensation course through my body. He said that Italy was always a place he had wanted to visit and it was only a couple of hours on an aeroplane and more so our son was old enough to appreciate his first trip on a plane as well.

It took weeks of persuading him to believe that I was scared of flying. I couldn't explain it was really just in case a passenger had the misfortune to be sick on the aeroplane or worse still, the chance that our son may vomit, seeing as he had never flown before. I was totally irrational but the whole mental and physical change in me was something so powerful I couldn't stop it.

Somehow I did convince him that driving would allow us to see other countries and it would be a huge part of our holiday.

OK so far so good until he mentioned if we were to drive then it would be best to catch the channel ferry and get as far as we could by sea to minimise the driving all the way to Venice.

So now I had a huge problem on my hands as the dreadful memories of the terrible journey we had to endure coming back from France sent me mentally spiralling out of control. I had a sort of ultimatum. It was fly or drive with the possibility of catching the ferry.

As my mind went into total overdrive I was determined to find a way which excluded boat and aeroplane. I took days working out easy routes on the map book and did several options of the cost of each. Eventually and triumphantly I planned a route that incorporated us using the Channel Tunnel and a direct route meaning we would drive all the way to Venice with a planned overnight stop. To my absolute joy my partner finally agreed and without any time for him to change his mind I booked the necessary tickets and accommodation.

We were lucky enough to have a soft top car at the time so the thought of having the roof down meant our son would be getting plenty of fresh air and minimise the risk of him feeling sick in the car. Although I will say he was an excellent traveller and loved going out in the car from a very young age.

For the first time in my life I had something to look forward too. I could happily boast that we were going abroad. I was totally ecstatic.

*   *   *

The journey was amazing. The channel tunnel was so easy and with the added bonus that all passengers have to stay in their vehicles was perfect for me. The thought that we were deep under the sea didn't even cross my mind although my partner did comment about it and how he didn't feel that comfortable. However within thirty five minutes we were emerging in the warm sunshine of France. Once abroad my thoughts were always about what we could safely eat and although I longed to be more adventurous and try local cuisine I could not risk the chance of contracting food poisoning so we stuck to more or less bread and cheese or visit the supermarket and I would cook. It didn't spoil our holiday at all as I would just convince my partner how much money we saved by cooking and doing our own catering as opposed to eating out all the time.

This holiday was such a success that we actually took another to France and also a trip to Prague and Germany in much the same way.

At last I felt that my phobia had not managed to ruin every aspect of my life. I could finally holiday like everyone else.

*   *   *

By now it was becoming more obvious to me that if the cause of vomiting was not from a contagious virus and could not be transmitted to me or my children I could deal with it in my own way, so when my youngest son started to suffer from tonsillitis with a fever making him sick due to his very high temperature, I was able to comfort him and coped in my own way, still calmed by brandy, and the fact that I wouldn't eat anything just in case was a revelation for me but at least I was coping, which was just as well as he eventually had to go into hospital and have his tonsils removed.

Unlike the years before when my eldest son had the same operation, this time I was able to take him into the hospital. His daddy came too for moral support but I do know my breakfast was a glass of brandy and nothing to eat. All that mattered to me was that I managed to do it and even more amazing was able to take him to the operating theatre with the nurse and stay with him while he was anesthetised.

When he was brought back to the ward he was groggy and I had a slight panicky feeling as I didn't know whether he was going to be sick or not but I made myself stay and look and act like all the other parents whose children had also been operated on that day.

He was allowed to come home the following day and recover at home. For me it was yet another step in the right direction to learning to live with my phobia, and just as well as a couple of years later in 1998 he was found to have a tumour in his leg which needed surgery and a lot of visits to Birmingham Oncology unit. On the day of his operation I had been given a parent's room to stay in as the system on the children's ward was that the parents would attend to their child's personal needs and the staff would only carry out the medical side of their recovery.

I did take my brandy with me and in the privacy of my room I did have a drink to keep me calm. I couldn't eat a lot I just snacked on peanuts, but our stay turned out to be a fun time for all. The children on the ward seemed to bounce back after their surgery. They only needed one day of sleeping then it was just like a big party with clowns and painting competitions, I could relax and enjoyed being just like all the other mums and dads.

*   *   *

By this time we had moved to Devon. My youngest son was now nine years old. My middle son was eighteen and had stayed with his father in Hampshire as he was working, and the eldest at twenty one had also secured a job as a flight attendant. I had muddled through their childhood and when I took time out to reflect how quickly the time had passed I had massive pangs of regret as to how I handled the whole issue of being a mother saddled with a massive phobia. I hated myself, tormented myself with the dread that my boys would have no love for me.

Fascinated by the fact that my eldest son had chosen a job as a flight attendant which in my mind put him in direct contact with a vomiting person if the flight was turbulent, I couldn't wait for him to visit us in Devon so I could ask him all sorts of questions to see what happened on the flights. It had now been twenty four years since I had been on an aeroplane and although I had no desire to go on one I was very curious in a morbid kind of way. I eventually did pluck up the courage and ask him what happens during the flight and how did passengers cope with the flight, finally getting to my question of passengers being sick. His answer astounded me when he said that during all of his flights not one passenger had vomited to his knowledge. He seemed curious to my question so when I explained about my last flight that I took way back in the 1970's he laughed and said 'oh mum, the aircraft have been modified over the years, you have to be very unlucky to get a flight so bad it will make you ill'. He loved the job and proved it as much by training and qualifying as a commercial pilot.

*   *   *

So for me once again life in general was good. My two older sons were both happy and had good jobs. The youngest son having made a full recovery from his medical problems was now able to realise his dearest wish to join the Army cadets, my husband was fully recovered from his terrible ordeal and I was back working in a building society, a job that I loved. However all was to be destroyed when my husband announced he wasn't happy with his lot. He was fast approaching his fortieth birthday and told me he wanted more out of life, was fed up with being 'in a rut' as he put it. I was devastated after all we had been through as a family I couldn't believe what was happening.

To spare any bad feelings and as it isn't relevant to my phobia I will skip to the point where sadly we are living separately in the same town with our son spending a week with his father and a week living with me. It was difficult but as long as our son stayed unaffected then it was to be for the best. Life carried on in general and I threw myself into my work. I had managed to achieve very good reports in the year of 2002 as a sales consultant and a lot of pressure was now on me to perform as well in 2003.

*   *   *

As I sit here typing and reliving my life I can now see for myself how I adapted my life so I avoided anything and everything connected with vomiting. I eliminated many things. Ridiculous things such as I have never been to a theme park as I wouldn't go on any of the rides just in case it made me sick. The most adventurous I have ever been is I did go on a big wheel once but that's it.

I would avoid using a lift not because that would make me sick but you see a person that was in the lift with me might just be sick.

One of most stupid occasions I can still remember is on a holiday with my parents when my first born son was around three months old. We visited North Devon and went to see the old cliff water railway at Lynton and Lynmouth. Any of you that have been there will know how steep the climb is and probably only takes about five minutes for the journey. I used the excuse I had the pram and walked it.

I would dearly love to go to a music concert but once again I worry too much about the person who would be standing next to me. What if they are drinking or on drugs and threw up. So I just pushed it out of my mind like many things I cut out of my life so it wouldn't cause me distress probably to the detriment of my family. So I wonder now if the breakup of my second marriage subconsciously gave me the nudge I needed to make the most of my life.

* * *

I finally started to have more of a social life and eventually started a friendship with a man. We were out having a quiet drink one evening when he told me his plans to live in abroad. I was intrigued by his visions and plans of how he was going to sell his home and move to live in the sun. In time he made his plans to visit Southern Spain and invited me to go with him as he had a friend who had accommodation that we could both use. Knowing that it would mean getting onto an aeroplane I inwardly panicked. Whether it was the wine I had drunk that evening or spurred on by what my son had told me or just a test to myself I agreed to go. Once the tickets were booked the realisation hit me that there was no way of escape now. I was going to take my first trip on an aeroplane for thirty years.

* * *

As the day fast approached I ate less and less. My stomach constantly churned with nerves and I must have made countless visits to the toilet, but I was also feeling a definite excitement about the situation.

As we had an early morning flight a very good friend of his invited us to stay overnight at his house and then offered drive us to the airport first thing in the morning.

I couldn't eat or drink a thing for nerve's, made sure I took a couple of travel sickness pills and had bought a bottle of rescue remedy hoping the combination would help me. Once we were booked in and in the departure lounge I really knew it was going to happen. I must have gone to the toilet about six times before our flight was called as I was determined that I would not be using the facilities on board the flight.

I asked to sit by the window as I didn't want a stranger sitting right next to me and my friend agreed as he knew that I hadn't been on a flight for years. I had told him that but not the reason behind it. He knew I was very nervous and once airborne ordered me the most welcoming glass of brandy to calm my nerves.

The flight was amazing. I loved looking out of the window and within a couple of hours we were preparing to land. No one to my knowledge had been ill, everyone seemed very much in a party mood and so they should be as they were all off on their well deserved holidays.

Stepping out into the warm sunshine I was elated and within an hour and a half we were sat drinking a cold beer overlooking the Mediterranean Sea. I couldn't stop smiling to myself I had turned a massive corner in my life and I knew now there was to be no turning back. We had the most wonderful week in Spain and I fell totally and utterly in love with the culture, the relaxed pace of life. For once I realised what I had been missing out on for all those years ago and how sad that I would never get the chance to go back to when I was sixteen and be able to start all over again.

All too soon our week came to an end. The good news was that my friend had made a conscious decision to relocate to Spain and had chosen a very nice luxury mobile home to eventually move into. The flight back to the UK was amazing and in just two hours we were back in the arrivals hall waiting for our luggage. His friend was waiting for us and as we drove back to his house he was eager to hear all the plans that my friend had made. All he had to do now was to sell his house.

Collecting my car I said my goodbyes and travelled back to North Devon and the solitude of my empty house. My young son had spent the week at his father's house and it had been agreed that he would come home from school on the Monday to me and spend the week with me. So Sunday was just a day of cleaning the house, catching up on the holiday washing, replying to emails and missed phone calls and getting myself back into work mode. It was more difficult than I realised and my mind kept wandering back to how beautiful Southern Spain was and joyfully I kept savouring the moment of pure exhilaration I felt when sat sipping my cold beer over-looking the sea. I had accomplished so much in a week. Experiencing two flights on an aircraft with no problems what so ever was to me the most amazing thing I had done for myself in a very long time.

*   *   *

Back at work everything suddenly seemed very stressful. My personal life was stressful, our divorce had been agreed and finalised but the sharing of my son was awful and still his father constantly seemed to wear me down.

As a financial sales consultant and assistant manager I had massive targets set out for me plus I had to motivate my work colleagues on a daily basis encouraging them to achieve their own personal targets. 2003 was in the financial world a nightmare. People didn't trust the economy and certainly weren't interested in investing their hard earned money in long term bonds. Every day became a struggle, and soon most days I found myself daydreaming that I was back on the beach, in the warm sunshine without a single care in the world.

The sound of my mobile phone bleeping with a text message bought me back to reality, even more so when it read that my friend had received an offer on his house and as far as he was concerned he was on his way to living in Spain. He came to visit the following weekend and constantly talked about his plans and what he was going to take with him and what he was selling. He was so wrapped up in the whole dream coming true I felt very envious. I suppose looking back I must have seemed very uninterested in his news and I think eventually he must have picked up on my misery and asking me why I poured out all my inner most thoughts (not my phobia) and feelings about my private life and my job and in reality how I couldn't see beyond the end of each day.

'Sell up and come with me then' are the only words he said to me. We sat and did the mathematics of how much cash I could realise from the sale of my home, added it to the amount of cash he was going to generate and the result was a fairly substantial sum of money. It would mean leaving my son behind with his father and saying goodbye to my family, but most of all, taking a massive personal risk as I would be sharing the same home as my friend but I or rather we believed it would work.

*   *   *

The following evening I telephone my ex-husband and asked if we could meet as I needed to talk to him. He invited me to his home which was more convenient as it was his turn to have our son stay with him for the week. With my stomach churning and my heart racing I told him of my friend's offer. Immediately he told me as far as he was concerned he didn't give a care as to my whereabouts in the world but there was absolutely no way that once I had made my choice that I would even be able have my son to stay with me anymore. Emotional blackmail or what?

Somehow though I just could not get the plan out of my head and a week later I visited the local estate agent with a view to putting my house on the market. Within two weeks I had sold to a family from Bath, looking for a family home in North Devon and more excitingly they paid the full asking price with no haggling. Signing the contracts I too was on my way to a new life albeit without my son. He was happy to be staying with his friends and family, and told me once he was old enough to fly unaccompanied that he was very lucky to have a nice holiday choice. At thirteen years of age he was a very understanding and considerate child. He had been very aware of the situation and the hostility between his father and me. I wonder if perhaps he was happy for me to be so far away hoping that I would be a happier person.

Giving in my notice at work proved more difficult. The higher management told me I was making a huge mistake and actually made my last working month quite uncomfortable. They moved me to my local tiny branch in my village with the reason that I would be closer to home and could pack up my belongings under less stress as I could walk to work in ten minutes rather than drive to the main town taking two hours out of my day.

*   *   *

Sorting out my belongings the truth and reality hit me like a brick wall. I hadn't questioned how we were going to get back to Spain. My answer came back to haunt me. We were to take the ferry from Plymouth to Santander. I was going to have to endure twenty four hours on a boat. Immediately I was transported back to that fateful journey twelve years ago. Panic and fear engulfed me. Suddenly I wanted to change my mind, but it was too late I had no choices, like the aeroplane journey I was going to have to face my fears head on.

Mid July and it's my last week in the UK. The removal lorry had just left my home with all our packing cases now on route to Spain. My son thankfully was staying with me until I left the UK as finally his father had acknowledged the fact that he could not control the situation by using blackmail tactics.

We had decided to take my car for the journey as it was quite big and enabled us to take the essential items needed to see us over the next couple of weeks. Our other belongings would take a while to be delivered at least three weeks. My emotions were running very high. I couldn't stop thinking about the boat journey and it was coming very close to having to say goodbye to my family.

*   *   *

Sat waiting in the car on the dockside queuing to board the ferry almost felt like a punishment for leaving behind all that was dear to me. Swallowing travel sickness pills like they were sweets didn't lessen my fears. I needed a large glass of brandy to do that. Once on board we found our cabin which was surprisingly very spacious with twin beds and our own bathroom. I felt more at ease knowing that I wouldn't have to use the public toilets on the ship with the worry of finding a sea sick passenger occupying one of the cubicles. Secondly if it all became too much and if the sea was rough I could escape to my own little sanctuary and not have to endure being surrounded by vomiting passengers. Just as the flight on the aeroplane I was going to be alright. I was going to be able to do this.

Standing up on the deck we watched as the ropes were finally released from the ship and that was it. We were on our way, with no going back. Watching the skyline of Plymouth grow smaller and smaller in the distance I felt the tears streaming down my face. In an instant it dawned on me that all I was doing was running away from my fears. In truth I was giving up being a proper mother to my teenage son. Ashamedly glad that I would not have to worry about whether he was going to be sick any more. Not have to worry that as he grew older he would try the drinking and smoking bit and come home drunk and vomit over the bathroom floor. The day I used to dream about when I would be on my own without any parental responsibilities had arrived. My parenting days had ended and with devastating results. Worse still I wasn't even in love with my man friend and he certainly wasn't in love with me. We were fond of each other but in all truthfulness we had used each other to realise totally different goals. As we made our way to the lounge I knew it was going to take more than a glass of brandy to get me through the next stage of my life.

*   *   *

The crossing was actually very pleasant I even managed a very small simple meal and happily spent the rest of the evening in one of the many lounges watching the onboard entertainment. I almost forgot we were on a ship. It was so very different to the nightmare crossing all those years ago.

Although I knew my feelings were not of love for this man I will be forever eternally grateful to him for unknowingly helping me through two massive and to a point terrifying situations in my life. He got me back on a plane and a ship.

*   *   *

As we sailed into Santander I could feel my excitement building. The sun was coming up and the warmth felt very comforting on my skin. Finally allowed to get into our car we couldn't wait to get out onto the road and start our long trek across Spain. We had planned it would take us at least two days to get to our destination so armed with a phrase book and map the next chapter in my life was just about to start.

Mid July and by now the sun is blazing over head. The car had threatened to overheat so we had to keep going with the temperature dial set to hot and try to keep cool by having all the windows wound down. All was well until we noticed we were in danger of losing some of our belongings out of the back windows. Reluctantly we had to wind them up and make do with the air as warm as it was coming through the front windows only. The closer we got to Madrid the hotter it became. By seven o' clock in the evening we had both taken as much as we could and found a small hotel to stay in for the night. With the aid of our book and a fellow customer we were able to book a room. Thankful to be out of the hot sun and in much need of a cool shower and cold water to drink we carried our bags to the room exhausted but happy that we were over half way of our journey.

After finding something to eat we made plans to get up very early and leave in the relative coolness of the early morning planning to reach our destination by midday and sure enough by eleven thirty to following morning we pulled up on the site that was to become our new home.

Over the following days we unpacked the car and put away the bits and pieces we had bought with us. Carried away by the newness and excitement of it all I forgot about my sadness and the guilt of leaving my family behind. We made quite a few friends and before long were part of a fairly large group of ex-pats. All of which had personal stories to tell of how they had arrived at the same site. Some had finally got their dreams of retiring in the sun. Others spent time between UK and Spain, the younger men on the site had evidently seen a small advertisement in an English newspaper offering the chance to live and work in the sun. The job being that the site had yet to be developed. It was all very basic and there was plenty of work for them. One thing though the holiday feeling was still very much evident amongst us all and gradually the trend was that we would all venture into the local town on a Saturday night and during the week someone would always be holding a BBQ to which everyone was invited.

August came and went and by now I had tanned for the first time in my life. I felt well, looked very well, had mastered the art of shopping in the local markets and supermarket, had found the natural spring where we were to go and collect our drinking water and even more excitingly my oldest son and his girlfriend had booked tickets to come and visit us for a week's holiday the first week of September.

We had a wonderful time although I did get a couple of phobia moments worrying that they may contract 'Spanish tummy' but all quite unnecessarily. They went home eager to report back to my family that I had made the right choice.

*   *   *

Within a couple of weeks we were indeed expecting more visitors. This time it was one of my man friend's daughters and her friend, booked to stay with us for two weeks. What a different holiday that proved to be. I suddenly felt like I was invisible. I felt used and nothing more than a general cook and cleaner. One evening it all got too much and I found myself in tears. Asking my friend why he was treating me in such a way he told me that his daughters, He has three were the most important people in his life. I was someone he had used basically I felt to swell the bank balance. For me it was over but felt trapped not only because I needed a roof over my head but I had just booked a ticket for my youngest son to visit us on his fourteenth birthday in October. He was allowed to fly as an unaccompanied minor. He was coming to see his mum.

In reality it was the thought of seeing my young son again that kept me strong and focussed every day. I would take myself off for walks along the beach or into the local town just to pass the time. It was very difficult to act as a couple in front of our friends as we were still expected to do the regular Saturday evening nights in the village as well as turn up at the impromptu BBQ's. The one drawback of living in a small community such as ours nothing seems to stay private. If they suspected that we were having problems they certainly didn't show it and as far as I am aware they didn't gossip about us either.

*   *   *

The day arrived when my son was due to arrive. He was scheduled to fly into Alicante at half past midnight. It was at least a two and a half hour journey to the airport from our site and fortunately for us we had an onsite taxi service which was regularly used for the other residents coming and going so it was arranged that my son could be met by the taxi and brought back to the site arriving around three o'clock in the morning. He looked so grown up when he arrived. I hadn't seen him for almost four months. I had really missed him.

We had a good week together and it was a welcome distraction from the reality of my crumbling life. The only unfortunate minor problem I had to overcome was that the poor lad did suffer a 'Spanish tummy' and was unexpectedly taken poorly on the beach. Whether it was because we were out in the open and I wasn't confined to a small space I don't know but I just got on and dealt with the situation and within twenty four hours he had completely recovered from his ordeal, and so had I.

Saying goodbye to him was the hardest thing. When we had parted prior to my moving to Spain he didn't show a huge amount of emotion. This time he cried his eyes out. I promised him I would come home for Christmas but it didn't lessen the pain. As he was driven away in the taxi I was racked with guilt and grief. Heartbroken at what I had done to my poor child. I couldn't bear to think of him getting on the aeroplane alone. How much more damage could I possibly bring about during my life.

Somehow we muddled through to Christmas. We were both flying back to the UK and had a flight booked for Late Christmas Eve. On arrival I was to visit my family and he was to visit his. We would eventually meet up on New Year's Eve before flying back to Spain a couple of days later. Even now as I look back it all seemed to pass in a haze. I had a great time with my family they all commented on how well I was looking and that the life obviously suited me. Little did they know the truth I had to just carry on keeping up the pretence of a wonderful life in the sun, and the benefits of real Mediterranean living.

*   *   *

Once back in Spain life became more difficult. My man friend I think suspected that I was considering a way out. I spent a lot of time alone and a lot of time talking to other residents on our site. The workmen were a good bunch of hard working people and I have to admit I enjoyed their company. I used to often just walk around the site or go and buy a newspaper hoping for a chance of a five minute chat with any of them. It was a welcome change for me the only down side of it was that my man friend started to become very possessive. He would want to know who I had seen, what we had chatted about, it all became very distressing. By now he wouldn't even socialise at the little bar by the communal pool so I started to go on my own as I knew there would always be a friendly face happy to sit and chat.

There was one person in particular who had become a good friend. At first he had been very stand offish when I had asked how he had ended up living on the site, but gradually he told me his life story and how he had been cheated on by his partner of many years. She had had an affair which culminated in her giving birth to another man's child. It was a very sad time for him resulting in losing all access to his own two children. I used to enjoy our chats and would look forward to seeing him most evenings. The only downside was I knew my man friend used to walk down to the bar and spy on me. It was all so childish and a bit frightening in reality.

By the end of January I had finally had more than I could take. February the ninth 2004 is a date etched in my brain forever. It was the day I made the best decision of my life. I walked into the office on our site. Explained my situation and within an hour I was sitting in my own little mobile home. I found the courage to confront my friend and insisted on him returning the money that was rightfully mine. It was sufficient to buy my own little place to live and leave me more than enough to carefully live on until I decided on my next move.

It was a bit embarrassing at first for us both really. He actually took it harder that I thought. Suddenly he had to look after himself and maybe it did him good I don't know but he gradually lost the three stones he had piled on since moving to Spain and having me cook and clean for him.

Me, on the other hand felt a mixture of relief, I was more than worried about what my future held, but I did make a conscious decision that I would not move back to the UK. I had come this far and I wasn't about to give up now. I continue to socialise amongst our group and to make a little money I learned to make beaded jewellery with the help of my neighbour which we then sold on site. We didn't make a fortune but it was enjoyable and a nice hobby that could be done sat by the pool or on the patio. We took quite a few orders in the summer months from visiting relatives of our friends. Life was pretty good and getting better all of the time as I had started to spend Saturdays with my new man who just happened to be . . . .

* * *

The workman who had openly told me his life story we found we had such a lot in common it was amazing. Within a few weeks I knew I had found my soul mate. He told me very much the same thing. After spending six years of his life in solitude I had finally restored his faith in the female species. He used to tell me of his hopes and dreams of re visiting America. He had travelled there when he was a teenager representing England in Basketball. He fell in love with the country, the people and the way of life. Even at fifteen he could see how the country held a certain magic, as if it really could make dreams come true. I was spellbound by his stories and by August we were making plans to visit a friend of his who lived in Texas. He was English and actually had a caravan sited on the site we were living on. He had recently married an American woman so now spent most of his time in America. One thing he did before leaving Spain was extended an invitation to my 'boyfriend' to visit him with the view to finding a job in the oil and gas industry, an industry well know to my boyfriend as he had worked for over ten years in the UK doing such a job.

By September we had booked tickets to visit his friend. I was now about to thoroughly test my phobia. I was going to take the longest flight for me ever. Ten hours in all and yet I knew I would do it. We had to fly to Gatwick from Spain. Stay overnight in one of the local motel's before catching our flight with Delta Airlines to Atlanta before connecting to an internal flight that would take us to our final destination Oklahoma. U.S.A.

* * *

I was mesmerised by the sheer enormity of the aircraft. I had only been used to the Airbus A320 that would hop from Spain to UK and now I was sat in this huge vessel. I know now that this was when I can put my hand on my heart and say with all honesty I fell in love with flying. After 30 years of refusing to contemplate taking any flight

I suddenly felt on top of the world. I wanted to cry for all the lost opportunities, my tears were though for the expectation and hopes my life was now offering up to me.

Most comforting to me though was amongst the hundreds of passengers on this flight I was not aware of anyone suffering with airsickness. My phobia was finally being laid to rest, at least with this part of the conquest. I was able to eat the food set in front of me. Confidently leave my seat to stretch my legs and visit the toilet.

*   *   *

Our plans were that once we arrived in Oklahoma we would collect a hire car and make our way to Texas and visit our friend and his wife. We had not arranged for any accommodation, deciding to drive until we found suitable overnight stops.

I was astounded by the vast open spaces and the roads which were absolutely straight. Not a bend or corner to be seen. With both of us transfixed by the sheer beauty of the landscape neither of us was aware of the speed in which we were travelling, until we passed a 'state trooper' sat in his patrol car. He had seen us though and before long was behind us flashing his blue lights. Hurriedly stopping the car my boyfriend got out with his passport and the car documents in his hands. I could see a long conversation was being held and finally he came back to the car smiling. Apparently when reminded of our speed my boyfriend had told the patrolman that we were so amazed by the sheer beauty of his glorious country he didn't notice how fast we were travelling. The patrolman was rather taken aback and thanked him saying he was proud to be an American then wished us to 'take care and have a good day'.

*   *   *

By day two we have found our friends house and spent a very enjoyable evening with them both. Before we left he gave my husband the name and address of an oil company we were to approach. The company was well known by our friend's wife's family so with huge hopes of a future in USA we said our fond farewells and made our way back to our motel.

We had to drive deep into the oil rich areas of America and our planned route was to take us past Roswell. My boyfriend had always had a massive interest in UFO's and of the history surrounding Roswell so you can imagine his excitement that we were to finally visit the town.

* * *

Our budget didn't allow for us to eat in every roadside diner and as I still was very wary about what I ate, just in case I contracted food poisoning we agreed to shop in the Walmart stores where the foods were very carefully prepared and packaged. What we didn't quite bargain for was the vast quantity of miles in between stores.

We had been driving for around four hours, were very hungry and in need of a visit to the toilet. Pulling up to a diner we went in and ordered coffee, which was very nice and complimentary. Knowing how big the meals can be we ordered one burger and chips unaware that American chips are not potato chips as we know it but more like thickly cut crisps.

Sharing the burger was more than enough for us and our coffee cups were replenished three more times as we ate our food. The waitress then offered extra chips as they too were complimentary only having to pay for the first basket full. She returned with a basket piled high. As naughty as it sounds I carefully stored these in my handbag to eat later in the day. What I didn't realise was that I was watched by a fellow customer who was sat at a table next to us. Feeling very embarrassed we left the correct money on the table and sneaked our way out of the diner.

Soon back on the road to Roswell, we couldn't stop laughing. We likened ourselves to a modern day Bonnie and Clyde. The wildlife we saw on our journey was fascinating, cheeky prairie dogs, plenty of smelly skunks, most of which were sadly road kill and unexpectedly quite a few armadillos. Haystack and Sardine mountains stood out proud on the horizon it was magical. I enjoyed following the maps and books we had purchased for our journey and loved the names these mountains had been blessed with. In reality it was all so over whelming, I could understand how the pull of the country can capture you so quickly.

*   *   *

I could write in detail every day of our trip as I did keep a daily journal. Maybe if I am successful in my quest in having this book published I could indeed write about our amazing journeys we have since made. You will read later on a little about how we have lived and worked in the States and Cyprus too but this book is not about this holiday but more about finally conquering my fear of getting on an aeroplane after thirty years due to my fear of being in close proximity of a vomiting passenger, and hopefully if any reader is stricken by the same fear, how I urge you to please overcome that fear and embrace the opportunity to travel before it's too late.

*   *   *

In total we spent a glorious five weeks driving seven thousand miles from Texas to Las Vegas where we married, (without the aid of Elvis) then back to Oklahoma city ready to return back to Spain blissfully happy and very excited about our future life together. During our travels we had visited several companies and visited several towns. Lovington was a small out of the way town that you wouldn't even know it existed but eventually was to provide us with amazing opportunities. We were taken in by a rich American family, fascinated by our story of looking for the opportunity to live and work in the USA. Unknowingly we had been 'adopted' by this very powerful family. The husband was an oil baron and the wife a member of the 'House of representatives' for the state of New Mexico as well as owning practically the whole of Lovington town.

In time we were both blessed with work offers. My new husband was to work for a huge treatment plant to do with oil, gas and water and I had been taken on in a newly built bank as a mortgage consultant. Confident in the knowledge we would apply with the aid of this family for our 'Green cards' our plans were taking shape. Time was going by far too quickly but we had accomplished what we had set out to do. Before we said goodbye to our new American family we discussed how we planned to support ourselves whilst waiting to complete all formalities appertaining to our work visas. It transpired the family owned the local Pizza restaurant. Intrigued that I did hold catering qualifications and had run my own establishment many years ago they offered us the opportunity to take over and run the restaurant as they were struggling to find competent staff. It all sounds too good to be true I know and we had to pinch ourselves several times. In reality all we had to do now was to return to Spain, sell our lovely little home and return. We had a temporary job to return to and the offer of an annex to their family home to live in until we had sorted out our future home.

*   *   *

October the 9th and we are back in Spain exhausted by our long journey, elated by the golden opportunities that lay ahead of us. I always believe in the saying 'fate always lends a hand' and this was most certainly the case for us. Our neighbours had relations staying with them for a holiday and also with a view to purchasing their own mobile home for a future retirement property. As we chatted to them about our trip we mentioned we would be selling up and moving to America. Yes, you guessed it the deal was sealed by first thing Monday morning. We sold everything to them. We were ecstatic and they were delighted with our or rather their new holiday/retirement home in the sun.

November 5th 2004 we say goodbye to all our friends in Spain and head off to the airport ready to start our new life in America. The last hurdle we have to cross is the fact we have to go to UK first and say our goodbyes to our respective families. Although we are very excited about starting our new life as a married couple in America our families are somewhat struggling with the reality of us being so far away. When living in Spain it was only a two and a half hour journey by aeroplane to be with us. However getting to our new home would involve three aeroplane flights and then a two hour drive from the final airport. It took twenty five hours to complete the journey and in my heart I knew that none of our elderly parents would be able to make the journey comfortably.

My husband's parents were the first to be visited. They live in North Wales which was pretty handy as I needed to visit Liverpool and change my passport into my new married name. After five lovely days we said our emotional goodbyes and set off to North Devon this time to my youngest son. At fifteen years of age he was fast turning into a lovely young man. He was still very much involved with the Army cadets and was due to march through the town in respect of Remembrance Sunday. I credited his father for taking good care of him since I moved out to Spain. We proudly watched his parade then taking my son with us we travelled on up to Hampshire to visit my parents and, also my two other son's.

After a few days all together we had to return my younger son back to his father in North Devon. It was a very sad and difficult time for all of us as we said our final goodbye. What I didn't expect was a torrent of abusive text messages from his father (my ex-husband) once he knew of my recent marriage and decision to move to America. Even after of our years apart he still felt he had the right to control my life.

Travelling back to my parents we called in to see my sister and her husband for a few hours finally arriving back at my parent's home later in the evening. The last two days were spent with my sons, their girlfriends and my parents.

Friday 19th November 2004. We had to leave my parents home by 4am in order to reach Gatwick in good time. Due to the spate of bombings in America we were required to check in at least three hours prior to departure. My poor dad was very emotional to the point he was ill. He couldn't even say the words goodbye. I felt terribly sad and guilty.

*   *   *

By the time we reached the airport I began to look forward to the flights. The first was to be to Atlanta in a huge 777 aircraft. One flight accomplished and two more to go we were required to pass through customs and complete our customary paperwork. We were soon waiting to board our next flight to Albuquerque. A three hour flight and on an aircraft similar to the type we used to fly between UK and Spain. Our journey was running like clockwork. One thing I will mention here is that not any time did I have the misfortune to witness anyone vomit. The public toilets in the airports were immaculate. I really have to ask myself the question why oh why did I have such horrible panic attacks in my younger years always expecting the worst. In reality apart from the few times I did have to deal with my phobia and the episodes already detailed in my story I can only re-iterate what a huge amount of wasted time I had spent imaging such horrors.

Our final flight was to be a short flight to Roswell in nothing more than a 'minibus' with wings a very small craft with no more than twenty seats. This was going to test me or so I thought. Blissfully I slept for the entire journey only waking up when we had landed. Taking a taxi cab to our motel we had made the journey safely, all we had to do now was collect our hire car in the morning and set out to find our adoptive family.

Our life in America was exciting our green cards were in the legal system. We purchased and renovated a little two bedroom bungalow. We spent happy days running the Pizza restaurant with plenty of laughs. I am sure half the customers only came to eat as they were fascinated by our English accents and our stories of why we were there. Our knowledge of the Spanish language proved to be very handy as living in the state of New Mexico meant we mixed with both Native Americans and those that had migrated from Mexico. It was a fascinating insight to their way of life. Until our green cards had been approved we had to travel out of America every ninety days. It was costly but we had to abide by the law. We used to make the journey back to UK to see our families. It did ease the pain somewhat.

It was to be almost a year after we first arrived when the bombshell was dropped by immigration shattering our dream world. It seems that every state has its own laws regarding immigrants. Unfortunately for us as we lived only an hour from the Mexican border it was all too easy for the Mexican families to visit the state usually with a heavily pregnant woman who would subsequently give birth in America thus giving them a legal right to be in the country.

Our phone call to advise us our green cards had been temporarily suspended for at least nine months (as had all immigrants coming into the state of New Mexico) was something we didn't see coming. Worse too was that if we abused our rights to be in the country we would be deported and refused future entry for up to ten years.

Within two weeks with the help of friends we had sold our home complete with food in the fridge. Devastated and with our dreams in tatters we made our desperately sad journey back to the UK. We were now without a home of our own and jobs. The only good thing we had to look forward to was the impending marriage of my eldest son and the celebration of my parents golden wedding anniversary, all of which was going to take place on the same weekend.

With just a week to go before my son's wedding we spent some time visiting my husband's parents who were very disappointed for us that our hopes and dreams were somewhat in tatters. We reassured them that we could start again and not to worry. We left with them feeling happier and returned to Hampshire for the big day. It was a joyous occasion and wonderful being back with my family again.

The day of the wedding passed very quickly and all too soon the evening was fast coming to a close. My youngest son wanted to stay on at the hotel with my other son and his friends with the promise they would return him to me in the morning ready to drive to the hotel to celebrate my parents golden anniversary. I didn't think to mention not to let him be stupid and drink too much, a big mistake.

*   *   *

On the morning of the golden anniversary party my younger son had still not arrived back at my parent's house. Thinking perhaps he had decided to travel down to the hotel with my other son we set out on the journey in the car with my parents. We had literally been gone about fifteen minutes when my mobile phone rang. It was my young son asking where we were. He was now back at my parent's home and not very well. It seems the other lads at the wedding thought it funny to lace his cokes with vodka. He had been very sick all night and was still vomiting. My panicky, hot and cold sweats and hammering heart engulfed me. This was just what I didn't want to deal with. When we got to my parents house he was crouched down vomiting on the grass verge. I was going to have to deal with this. I reasoned he was sick because of excessive drinking and it wasn't contagious. I was not going to end up vomiting myself. My parents dropped us off and we told them to go to the hotel to welcome their guests. We would deal with the problem of my son and travel down in our hire car.

I wanted to leave him at my parent's home in bed. I didn't want to be in the car with him while he continued to vomit. Just like all those years ago when I was a little eight year old girl. The thought of being trapped in the car was more than I could cope with. I hated him. I shouted at him saying all sorts of irrational things. I couldn't stop the words tumbling out of my mouth. I hated my other son's for allowing it to happen. All the good thoughts of me having somewhat gotten over my phobia disappeared in a puff of smoke. I was back to being that horrible, sweaty panicky person. I wanted to just walk away and leave him.

He must have sensed my anxiousness and I know felt guilty at knowing he had to a point abused my trust especially as we had another important event to attend to with my celebrating parents. When I continued to rant and rave at him telling him he had to stay at home in bed on his own I must admit he cried. At sixteen years old I had made him cry with my horrible attitude. My husband intervened in the end and suggested we help him get freshened up make him comfortable in the back of the car complete with a plastic bowl in case of any further vomiting, let him sleep it off and carry on with the day.

The journey was a nightmare. At first we stopped the car every time he wanted to be sick, however once on the main roads there came a point that we couldn't stop in time. He vomited in the car. Here I was without realising it I was actually confronting the very same issue that set my phobia in action all those years ago. After he had been sick in his bowl in the car I felt calm. I had dealt with my phobia. We eventually arrived at the hotel and left my son in the car to sleep.

My other son's were very apologetic they didn't realise quite how much the poor boy had been given to drink. Thankfully it didn't spoil a beautiful celebratory day for my parents. Most of the guests at the party had been at my son's wedding and found the story of my drunken son amusing. Most went out to the car to see how he was taking cold water for him to sip as well as words of sympathy.

After a wonderful day it was time to make the return journey back to my parent's home. By now my son was feeling a little better and ate a banana and managed to drink a large glass of water. Half way home and he vomited everything up into his bowl in close proximity to me in the car. I didn't panic I actually coped. My husband stopped the car so I could clean his bowl and we carried on home. Inside I felt a huge sense of relief I had finally confronted my demon.

* * *

With all the excitement over it was time for us to make a decision as to our next steps in life. We had all our worldly goods contained in four suitcases and our precious family pictures and photographs packaged up into a huge parcel. The hopes of a future in America were slim and the possibilities of finding work opportunities back in Spain would prove to be fruitless. It was time to consider our next move. We spent the next few days ensconced in the library. Pouring over information books and trawling the internet researching every country that was within the European Union which would make it easier for us to find work.

Cyprus proved to be the most popular choice for us. The English language was freely spoken, they had recently become part of the EU we decided we had nothing to lose by taking a trip to visit the Island. We booked a very cheap package deal for a two week trip. We would be allocated our hotel or apartment on arrival our hopes were slightly raised.

The following week we found ourselves in Protaras which is fairly close to Aiya Napa. The weather was perfect it was early June and we had been allocated an apartment overlooking Fig Tree Bay. We felt like we were in heaven it was beautiful. The first thing we had to do was to find a hire car we reminded ourselves this was a working holiday and our last chance to sort our future life.

The funds finally arrived from America from the sale of our little house so we were able to open a bank account. Within a week we had found an apartment to rent and my husband applied for a job.

With our hopes of making a future in Cyprus we drove back to Larnaca airport and found a holiday representative from the company we had travelled with. You should have seen the look on her face when we told her that we would not be on the flight back to UK. It was a picture. After confirming our decision again and again she accepted our choice.

Incredibly my husband got the job which was just as well as it was the only one available. He was to start working in the September so we spent the entire summer together getting our little home established. Two of my sons came to visit. It was a wonderful time of our lives. We couldn't believe our luck. The only little problem we had was that we did finally have to relocate to Paphos in September as that was where my husband had to travel to work. We managed it. The funny thing was that as he had already started work it was down to me to move home as he could not take time off. So on the day of our move he went to work I packed up our possessions with the help of a removal company and moved to the other end of the Island. We had only viewed the property once but with the help of a few phone calls I managed to find our new home. My poor husband on the other hand spent ages driving round and round trying to find me. I did laugh when he phoned me saying he was lost. I found him eventually. Once again we had dropped to a tiny part of the world and created a new life for ourselves. We often used to joke with each other and say we should design a television programme whereby you give the contestants a small sum of money and drop them somewhere in the world and track their progress over the course of a year. We always said we would win.

As I have already mentioned when talking about our life in America this book is not really about our lives as such but more about my journey through life saddled with my soul destroying Phobia. I did have occasions in Cyprus that I had to deal with situations. Mainly my younger son, who by now is an adult and serving in the British Army, he frequently used to come and visit me usually with a friend in tow. Boys will be boys as we all know and they used to go off and drink far too much resulting in my son always vomiting. I am not sure whether the thought of me shouting at him has imprinted in his mind but he always used to go into the field opposite our house rather than use the bathroom.

*   *   *

Due to the line of work my husband undertook we spent five wonderful years in Cyprus. He worked hard at being part of a team constructing a world class golf course. We were both very heavily involved with a Dog rescue centre I was the treasurer as well as a cleaner, all on a voluntary basis and my husband helped with the construction of their new shelter.

With our life progressing beyond all our wildest dreams there was just one dream I wanted to turn into a reality.

You see when the world greeted the year 2000 my parents and my sister and her family all celebrated together in Disneyworld Florida. I never disclosed to anyone how jealous I was. I was jealous of the fact they could just get on a plane without any fear. It was all I had ever wanted to do but at that time it was to me only ever going to be a dream. The only person I ever told in my life is my husband. He is the only person that I ever told that I had a phobia.

So now having conquered my fears of being trapped in aeroplane surrounded by vomiting travellers and having managed several long haul flights to America when we lived there in 2004 it was suddenly a possibility.

March 2009. Finally and excitedly we booked our dream holiday to Florida. We were to spend almost three weeks living the dream. We were to travel in style on a 747 with business class seats in the upstairs area of the plane. I was to finally get my dream of going to see Disneyworld. My husband in turn got his dream of visiting NASA space station and it was on this holiday that I pushed myself and actually went in a simulator. Doesn't sound like a big deal to the normal person but this took every ounce of concentration to get in it. We were in groups of four and our mission was to pilot the vessel to Mars.

Standing in the queue we were grouped with a mother and her ten year old child. I was very panicky, sweating with fear and to make it worse as we sat in the vessel the voice commander that we had to listen to for our instructions just had to mention the sick bags. I wanted to get off there and then but the harness automatically held me in place. I sat with my eyes shut the feeling that these simulators can are amazing I will say that. The force of the take off the feeling of weightlessness it was all very clever but I was very glad to get off but at the same time I had pushed myself or rather my husband pushed my limits and I am glad he did.

We flew to the Bahamas and swam with the dolphins and played with sealions in the Florida Keys. I even got my first tattoo of a dolphin in celebration at the age of 51. We had the most glorious time. It was magical and a true celebration of our wonderful life together and of the realisation that I had to a point accomplished many simple everyday things that contributed towards helping me conquer my phobia.

Once my husband's contract had finished he was required to move onto his next project in yet another part of the world. I had the choice of staying in Cyprus or moving on. As it was we finally decided to buy an old farmhouse back in Spain, only half an hour from where we used to live and where we first met. For me I was finally going home.

I left Cyprus June 2010. My husband had already moved on to Portugal and it was up to me to hand over our home, say goodbye to our huge circle of friends and hardest of all I had to transport me and our six dogs from Cyprus to Spain. It was one of the most emotionally difficult things I ever had to do on my own. I knew I had to cope. It took from 8.30pm on the Sunday night until 03.30am Tuesday morning to complete my journey. I did it all with the aid of just a couple of travel sickness pills and a whole load of sheer determination and willpower.

*   *   *

You may wonder what my life is like now and if I am still affected by my Phobia.

I am extremely happy I love my life although I still have many limitations as to what I will subject myself to. I know as much as I would love to go on a cruise I doubt if it will ever happen. My reasons though are nothing to do with being sea-sick or rather fellow passengers suffering it's the simple fact you see that I have read in the newspapers and seen the news reports on the television about how cruise ships can carry secret demons. How it only takes one passenger to carry a germ onboard. How the other passengers can unknowingly contract the vomiting bug once onboard and how quickly it manifests itself amongst the other passengers. I read about one such ship that had to dock but no-one was allowed off the ship. That would be my living nightmare. The classic feeling of being trapped surrounded by germ infested people and with no way of getting away from the situation. Nowhere to run, nowhere to hide, sitting in a ticking time bomb. That's the picture that comes into my head and induces the classic hot and cold sweats, a dry mouth and thumping heart, just by reading and visualising the scene.

Equally as bad is when it is reported in the newspapers about the winter vomiting bug (Norovirus) that affects the UK during the winter months, and how the hospitals are massively affected as well as entire areas of the country. I always try to visit my family around Christmas time. As you now know I have made massive progress and will travel on my **own** to the UK to visit my family. I still take two travel sickness pills and sip drops of rescue remedy to get on the flight and will sometimes have a brandy during the flight. I can do this and that is so wonderful but what always niggles at me is the question has the winter vomiting bug affected anyone on the aircraft. It is always the fear of the unknown that I struggle with. However as soon as I am off the aircraft and with my family these thoughts fade away and I have a wonderful time.

Looking back I know that eventually I did achieve holidays abroad with my youngest son. I would have loved to have been able to take my children on an aeroplane. I am just grateful to my parents. They did that for me, blissfully unaware of my phobia and took my two older children skiing in the winter and to Corfu in the summer as well as some very happy camping holidays in the West Country when they were quite young.

All I have are photographs stored away in albums at my parent's house. Hopefully my children do have the memories of good fun holidays spent on our little boat and hope they don't feel they missed out on holidays abroad sadly not shared with their mum and dad. There is a particular advertisement on the television at the moment for Disney world. That advert and the reactions of the children how they whoop with joy and excitement running into the arms of their parents sharing such happy times is what I know I have missed out on. Every time I see it I get a huge lump in my throat. I was very envious of my sister as she has travelled with her children when they were younger and has shared many wonderful holidays with her children as they grew up.

*   *   *

A classic example of my mental attitude to this odd phobia is just the other day my parents came to visit me in Spain and whilst on our journey home I asked how their flight was and in general it was a good flight, good seats etc and then mum said to my dad 'did you see that girl in front of you being sick?' she carried on 'well it was when you were eating your sandwich'. He hadn't and wasn't bothered by it any way.

As she spoke I instantly got the panicky feeling and this is what went around in my head.

Did she have a germ or sickness bug, had she breathed all her germs into the air system on the plane, had my parents breathed in the germs, were they now possibly carrying a bug, were they going to be ill and worse still was I going to catch it. That is how my mind still works.

I try to reason with myself and the possibility of this all happening. I concentrate on inwardly asking or telling myself of the other reasons that she was sick. She could be pregnant, she could have possibly had too much to eat or drink the previous evening. It all seems so ridiculous and by the time we had arrived home it was forgotten.

However later that evening when we were relaxing with a drink and chatting I did tell them that I am writing this book and I did tell them my mental reactions to their conversation in the car. If only to try and explain what living with this phobia can still do to me and how my mental state becomes over active and irrational.

I am doing my very best to fight the damage as I want to be able to have fun with my grandchildren, to make amends to my own children through theirs. Just to be able to cuddle them, have fun, and, as they grow older be able to bring them to Spain to stay for holidays with me, I just want to be a proper loving grandmother and not someone who keeps them at arm's length.

I promise you I am much better, although I wish could still have some help I will admit to that. My dream would to be possibly treated with some sessions of hypnosis therapy if it is possible, as opposed to the counselling that was offered to me all those years ago, that still makes me shudder to think what I may have to endure.

*   *   *

I know I have adapted a way of living daily but it is under my terms I suppose and it gets me happily through my days. I wash up with water that is almost boiling to the point it will burn my hands through rubber gloves but I feel happy knowing that my cutlery and crockery is clean. I am very careful of food storage and cooking. Any leftover food normally gets given to my dogs as I am never too keen to reheat food for fear of making myself ill.

I always bleach everything even though it is only me and my dogs living in the house as my husband works away from home only getting back here once every eight weeks just for a week. One point is he has in a good way picked up a good cleaning and cooking regime from me and proved it just the other day by telling me his work colleagues had all been ill, probably due to something they had eaten out at the local cafe. He was the only one not to join them preferring to go back to his house to cook at home. So at least some good has come of it . . .

I will and do avoid eating out as much as possible. For example, most Friday's it is common practice for a group of us to meet at the local tapas bar for coffee and tapas after our morning shopping at the local market. I always decline the opportunity to eat but I admit I watch in envy as they tuck into the different foods. My reason being is that tapas are stored on the counter sometimes under cover but not always. If required they are reheated in the microwave but to me that's just asking for trouble. I will say though that my friends do have something to eat every week and none have mentioned they have been ill. So yes I should get over it and try one. Maybe I will one day, but at the moment I am happy to just sit in the sunshine with my coffee, although on the positive side I have found two establishments here in Spain that I have eaten at several times and thoroughly enjoyed the food so all is not lost

When my parents come to visit they love to do the shopping. They both love to sample the local foods and follow a more Mediterranean diet. Doing such a shop my dad picked up a packet of crab sticks. I know there was nothing odd in that except, it wasn't my normal food that I eat due to eliminating shellfish from my diet I simple refused to try one.

Eventually I did taste one and happily and really quite obviously didn't vomit from this different food I now love them. I didn't realise how nutritious they were and a very good source of omega 3 oil and always have a packet in my fridge. The same was when my dad went wandering off in the supermarket and came back rather pleased with himself as he had mastered his best Spanish and bought a kilo of fresh sardines. I made myself eat them and thoroughly enjoyed them even returning for a second plateful.

I know I am very careful about what I eat. Realistically my training in catering and hospitality has educated my mind as to the rights and wrongs of food storage whereas my one bout of food poisoning all those years ago has imprinted on my mind and has taken some of the pleasure of eating out in restaurants. I know that will never change. If I do eat out it has to be at a place that I have eaten at before and with no bad effects. I limit the food I choose and usually stick to something simple. Avoiding chicken as it really has to be stored and cooked properly plus all types of shellfish. Sounds mad to an outsider but I can't help it. Why shellfish you may wonder. Simple, I went to a birthday party a couple of years ago and a colleague of mine chose to eat the mussels as they were her favourite treat. She was very ill for a few days afterwards and said at the time she felt like she was going to die. So that did it for me another choice of food dismissed in my mind.

*   *   *

As for the other issues I used to struggle with. Now I will make myself walk past a patch of vomit on the pavement, although the other day I happened to be out shopping and was about to cross the road when I notice a young woman bent down by the side of the road. She was vomiting and I literally froze on the spot. I needed to walk past her but couldn't do until she had finished and gone. When she stood up she was very heavily pregnant and so I could reason with myself that she was probably suffering due to her being pregnant and not carrying some sort of bug. Never the less I still held my breath as I walked past the spot where she had been, but I felt compelled to see where she had vomited. Each week I passed the same place I had to look to see if the mess was still there. Why I don't know but at least I could look at it and walk past it.

Now this was the first time that I can remember for simply ages, years in-fact, since I have seen someone be sick out in public and then just only last week I had been collecting a hire car to use when another holiday hire car pulled in not far from where I was standing. A young boy got out and vomited. He was or I told myself it was only travel sickness, nothing that could harm me and as much as I wanted to move away I couldn't as the member of staff dealing with me was talking me through the car details. I survived.

Shopping, I am so much better and I certainly don't spend or rather waste time finding the empty Isles. I can say with my hand on my heart I actually enjoy shopping. I love to visit the outdoor markets as well as the supermarkets. I don't actually give any thought or waste any time waiting for something to happen. I can see now what a ridiculous amount of time I have wasted over the years. Life is far too precious for me now and aim to make the most of every day.

In all if I take a good long look back at the amount of precious time I have wasted over this phobia it makes me feel so angry with myself, frustrated and yet so terribly sad. I feel horrible and terribly ashamed when I think back to when my children were small, how I never used to kiss them very much. Maybe on the head or face but never on the lips or near their mouth's only because I always worried they may be harbouring germs in their saliva. Even a cuddle was somewhat restricted. I couldn't have their face to close to mine. I have huge regrets and have to live with these regrets every day.

To think that I have coped with three miscarriages, three children born and raised, major surgery to include a full hysterectomy plus countless other procedures, and not once have I vomited ever since my first miscarriage over thirty years ago. All I can say is what a terrible waste of time my worrying was.

On the positive side I have now travelled extensively as well as lived and worked in various parts of the world all with absolutely no ill effects what so ever.

* * *

I am glad I have begun to open up and be frank about my situation, I felt ridiculously embarrassed at first and found it very difficult to actually get the words out and tell people, but amazingly just the other day I happened to be chatting on Skype with a friend. We both used to live in Cyprus and have kept in touch since she returned to the UK and I moved back here to Spain. Keen to know what I have been doing with my time she asked and I mentioned my magazine article that was to be published. I explained to her how I needed to highlight the horrors of this phobia and how important it was to somehow stop any other sufferers from going through the same pain and anguish as myself. So you can imagine how I felt when she told me her daughter-in-law is currently suffering very much in the same way and although she has a young son she is battling against the phobia every day to the point where she may put off having another child as she doesn't think she will or can cope.

Just by being more open I have discovered that I am not the only one saddled with this problem.

*   *   *

Earlier this week I travelled to another part of Spain for an overnight stop with my eldest son, my daughter-in-law and her parents and her sister and husband and my darling little grandson. They were all enjoying a big family holiday for a week. I hadn't seen my daughter-in-law's family for six years since my son's wedding and due to the fact that I had been living abroad in Cyprus.

During the day it was announced that my daughter-in-laws's sister was pregnant with her first child. Of course I was delighted for her but I felt compelled to ask if she was well or suffering from morning sickness. Selfishly I needed to know, as long as I knew I would condition myself, thankfully for her she had not suffered at all and for me, yes very selfishly I could sit back and relax.

Living abroad has had for me huge drawbacks in that I haven't spent a lot of time with my grandchildren. When I lived in Cyprus I ran my own business boarding dogs and time off was very limited. Now I live in Spain I plan to have more time with my family. Understandably with this visit my young grandson didn't really know who I was. It was only the third time I had seen him since he was born. The first time he was only three weeks old and the last time was at Christmas just for a few hours at a family gathering, so you can imagine my delight when he toddled over and reached out for my hand to take him to go and play a game on the pool table. He only wanted to mess round and put the balls in the nets but I felt wanted by this tiny person.

In the afternoon I went to the beach with my son, daughter-in-law and my little grandson. He loved it rolling in the warm sand, playing on the slide and running to me and catching hold of my hand. This is all I ever wanted for me with my own children. I felt on top of the world. He loves me and I am his Nana . . . .

Later that evening my daughter-in-law and her mum and myself were all sat outside talking and drinking wine. I mentioned that I had an article that was going to be published in a magazine about my phobia about people vomiting and more my fear of vomiting, and how I had kept it a secret for forty six years. I needed to explain as my daughter-in-law was to be mentioned as was her young son, my grandson in the article.

Our conversation then turned to my problem and it was mentioned how they noticed I questioned her sister about morning sickness. My daughter-in-law then revealed that she had a female friend who suffered from the same phobia and how she wouldn't hold my grandson just in case he vomited on her. Worse still she is just about to get married has said many times she doesn't think she could cope with having any children as she would not be able to cope with the problem if they were ill and vomited.

I wanted so much to cry for this lovely young girl. With a whole life ahead of her she was already a prisoner to this horrible phobia. To miss out on having the chance of a family and all the joy it should bring. I just hope that she will overcome her fears and maybe if this book is published she will take some sort of comfort from it. I would advise her firstly not to hide the fact she is a sufferer, although she has talked about it to my daughter-in-law. Be open and honest and above all have the courage to get professional help.

So you see I have discovered two young women who are technically within my circle of acquaintances, and yet I never knew. The good point is though that they both have admitted to it whereas I couldn't for fear of looking stupid. If I could have just one wish it would be for these two young women who still have a lifetime in front of them, to get help and see it through till the end. Have the precious gift of children and love them without limits.

My day and evening with my family passed all too quickly and after a leisurely breakfast the following morning it was soon time for me to start my four hour journey back to my home. My little grandson was very tired and needing his mid morning nap. He was in his daddy's arms at the time and I just needed to say goodbye to him. The most magical thing was for him to come to me, as sleepy as he was, wrapped in my arms I hugged him. Taking out his dummy I asked him for a kiss goodbye for his Nana and with that he put his little face up to mine and I kissed him on his little soft damp lips. It was the sweetest little kiss in the whole wide world . . . .

www.ingramcontent.com/pod-product-compliance
Lightning Source LLC
Chambersburg PA
CBHW030406290526
45785CB00004B/1915